Far Out

Far Out

Edited by
Arthur J. Arkley

NELSON

THOMAS NELSON AND SONS LTD
Nelson House Mayfield Road
Walton-on-Thames Surrey KT12 5PL
51 York Place
Edinburgh EH1 3JD
P.O. Box 18123 Nairobi Kenya

Yi Xiu Factory Building
Unit 05-06 5th Floor
65 Sims Avenue Singapore 1438

THOMAS NELSON (HONG KONG) LTD
Toppan Building 10/F 22A Westlands Road
Quarry Bay Hong Kong

THOMAS NELSON (NIGERIA) LTD
8 Ilupeju Bypass PMB 21303 Ikeja Lagos

First published in 1974
Reprinted 1975, 1976, 1979, 1982, 1983

Selection © Thomas Nelson and Sons Ltd 1974
ISBN 0-17-432055-8
NCN 220-2616-5

Cover design by Jill Leman
Cover photograph by Barnaby's Picture Library

Printed in Hong Kong

Contents

For Eileen
who keeps a sense of wonder

The Secret

Henry Cooper had been on the Moon for almost two weeks before he discovered that something was wrong. At first it was only an ill-defined suspicion, the sort of hunch that a hardheaded science reporter would not take too seriously. He had come here, after all, at the United Nations Space Administration's own request. UNSA had always been hot on public relations—especially just before budget time, when an overcrowded world was screaming for more roads and schools and sea farms, and complaining about the billions being poured into space.

So here he was, doing the lunar circuit for the second time, and beaming back two thousand words of copy a day. Although the novelty had worn off, there still remained the wonder and mystery of a world as big as Africa, thoroughly mapped, yet almost completely unexplored. A stone's throw away from the pressure domes, the labs, the spaceports, was a yawning emptiness that would challenge men for centuries to come.

Some parts of the Moon were almost too familiar, of course. Who had not seen that dusty scar in the Mare Imbrium, with its gleaming metal pylon and the plaque that announced in the three official languages of Earth:

ON THIS SPOT
AT 2001 UT
13 SEPTEMBER 1959
THE FIRST MAN-MADE OBJECT REACHED ANOTHER WORLD

Cooper had visited the grave of Lunik II—and the more famous tomb of the men who had come after it. But these things belonged to the past; already, like Columbus and

7

the Wright brothers, they were receding into history. What concerned him now was the future.

When he had landed at Archimedes Spaceport, the Chief Administrator had been obviously glad to see him, and had shown a personal interest in his tour. Transportation, accommodation, and official guide were all arranged. He could go anywhere he liked, ask any questions he pleased. UNSA trusted him, for his stories had always been accurate, his attitude friendly. Yet the tour had gone sour; he did not know why, but he was going to find out.

He reached for the phone and said: 'Operator? Please get me the Police Department. I want to speak to the Inspector General.'

Presumably Chandra Coomaraswamy possessed a uniform, but Cooper had never seen him wearing it. They met, as arranged, at the entrance to the little park that was Plato City's chief pride and joy. At this time in the morning of the artificial twenty-four-hour 'day' it was almost deserted, and they could talk without interruption.

As they walked along the narrow gravel paths, they chatted about old times, the friends they had known at college together, the latest developments in interplanetary politics. They had reached the middle of the park, under the exact centre of the great blue-painted dome, when Cooper came to the point.

'You know everything that's happening on the Moon, Chandra,' he said. 'And you know that I'm here to do a series for UNSA—hope to make a book out of it when I get back to Earth. So why should people be trying to hide things from me?'

It was impossible to hurry Chandra. He always took his time to answer questions, and his few words escaped with difficulty around the stem of his hand-carved Bavarian pipe.

'What people?' he asked at length.

'You've really no idea?'

The Inspector General shook his head.

'Not the faintest,' he answered; and Cooper knew that he was telling the truth. Chandra might be silent, but he would not lie.

'I was afraid you'd say that. Well, if you don't know any more than I do, here's the only clue I have—and it frightens me. Medical Research is trying to keep me at arm's length.'

'Hmm,' replied Chandra, taking his pipe from his mouth and looking at it thoughtfully.

'Is that all you have to say?'

'You haven't given me much to work on. Remember, I'm only a cop; I lack your vivid journalistic imagination.'

'All I can tell you is that the higher I get in Medical Research, the colder the atmosphere becomes. Last time I was here, everyone was very friendly, and gave me some fine stories. But now, I can't even meet the Director. He's always too busy, or on the other side of the Moon. Anyway, what sort of man is he?'

'Dr Hastings? Prickly little character. Very competent, but not easy to work with.'

'What could he be trying to hide?'

'Knowing you, I'm sure you have some interesting theories.'

'Oh, I thought of narcotics, and fraud, and political conspiracies—but they don't make sense, in these days. So what's left scares the devil out of me.'

Chandra's eyebrows signalled a silent question mark.

'Interplanetary plague,' said Cooper bluntly.

'I thought that was impossible.'

'Yes—I've written articles myself proving that the life forms on other planets have such alien chemistries that they can't react with us, and that all our microbes and bugs took millions of years to adapt to our bodies. But I've always wondered if it was true. Suppose a ship has come back from Mars, say, with something *really* vicious—and the doctors can't cope with it?'

There was a long silence. Then Chandra said: 'I'll start investigating. *I* don't like it either, for here's an item you probably don't know. There were three nervous breakdowns in the Medical Division last month—and that's very, very unusual.'

He glanced at his watch, then at the false sky, which seemed so distant, yet which was only two hundred feet above their heads.

'We'd better get moving,' he said. 'The morning shower's due in five minutes.'

The call came two weeks later in the middle of the night —the real lunar night. By Plato City time, it was Sunday morning.

'Henry? Chandra here. Can you meet me in half an hour at air-lock five? Good—I'll see you.'

This was it, Cooper knew. Air-lock five meant that they were going outside the dome. Chandra had found something.

The presence of the police driver restricted conversation as the tractor moved away from the city along the road roughly bulldozed across the ash and pumice. Low in the south, Earth was almost full, casting a brilliant blue-green light over the infernal landscape. However hard one tried, Cooper told himself, it was difficult to make the Moon appear glamorous. But nature guards her greatest secrets well; to such places men must come to find them.

The multiple domes of the city dropped below the sharply curved horizon. Presently, the tractor turned aside from the main road to follow a scarcely visible trail. Ten minutes later, Cooper saw a single glittering hemisphere ahead of them, standing on an isolated ridge of rock. Another vehicle, bearing a red cross, was parked beside the entrance. It seemed that they were not the only visitors.

Nor were they unexpected. As they drew up to the dome, the flexible tube of the air-lock coupling groped out towards them and snapped into place against their tractor's outer hull. There was a brief hissing as pressure equalised. Then Cooper followed Chandra into the building.

The air-lock operator led them along curving corridors and radial passageways towards the centre of the dome. Sometimes they caught glimpses of laboratories, scientific instruments, computers—all perfectly ordinary, and all deserted on this Sunday morning. They must have reached the heart of the building, Cooper told himself when their guide ushered them into a large circular chamber and shut the door softly behind them.

It was a small zoo. All around them were cages, tanks, jars containing a wide selection of the fauna and flora of Earth. Waiting at its centre was a short, grey-haired man, looking very worried, and very unhappy.

'Dr Hastings,' said Coomaraswamy, 'meet Mr Cooper.'

The Inspector General turned to his companion and added. 'I've convinced the Doctor that there's only one way to keep you quiet—and that's to tell you everything.'

'Frankly,' said Hastings, 'I'm not sure if I give a damn any more.' His voice was unsteady, barely under control, and Cooper thought, Hello! There's another breakdown on the way.

The scientist wasted no time on such formalities as shaking hands. He walked to one of the cages, took out a small bundle of fur, and held it towards Cooper.

'Do you know what this is?' he asked abruptly.

'Of course. A hamster—the commonest lab animal.'

'Yes,' said Hastings. 'A perfectly ordinary golden hamster. Except that this one is five years old—like all the others in this cage.'

'Well? What's odd about that?'

'Oh, nothing, nothing at all . . . except for the trifling fact that hamsters live for only two years. And we have some here that are getting on for ten.'

For a moment no one spoke; but the room was not silent. It was full of rustlings and slitherings and scratchings, of faint whimpers and tiny animal cries. Then Cooper whis-

11

pered : 'My God—you've found a way of prolonging life!'

'No,' retorted Hastings. 'We've not found it. The Moon has given it to us . . . as we might have expected, if we'd looked in front of our noses.

He seemed to have gained control over his emotions—as if he was once more the pure scientist, fascinated by a discovery for its own sake and heedless of its implications.

'On Earth,' he said, 'we spend our whole lives fighting gravity. It wears down our muscles, pulls our stomachs out of shape. In seventy years, how many tons of blood does the heart lift through how many miles? And all that work, all that strain is reduced to a sixth here on the Moon, where a one-hundred-and-eighty-pound human weighs only thirty pounds.'

'I see,' said Cooper slowly. 'Ten years for a hamster—and how long for a man?'

'It's not a simple law,' answered Hastings. 'It varies with the size and the species. Even a month ago, we weren't certain. But now, we're quite sure of this : on the Moon, the span of human life will be at least two hundred years.'

'And you've been trying to keep it secret!'

'You fool! Don't you understand?'

'Take it easy, Doctor—take it easy,' said Chandra softly.

With an obvious effort of will, Hastings got control of himself again. He began to speak with such icy calm that his words sank like freezing raindrops into Cooper's mind.

'Think of them up there,' he said, pointing to the roof, to the invisible Earth, whose looming presence no one on the Moon could ever forget. 'Six billion of them, packing all the continents to the edges—and now crowding over into the sea beds. And here—' he pointed to the ground—'only a hundred thousand of *us*, on an almost empty world. But a world where we need miracles of technology and engineering merely to exist, where a man with an I.Q. of only a hundred and fifty can't even get a job.

'And now we find that we can live for two hundred years. Imagine how they're going to react to *that* news! This is

12

your problem now, Mister Journalist; you've asked for it, and you've got it. Tell me this, please—I'd really be interested to know—*just how are you going to break it to them?*

He waited, and waited. Cooper opened his mouth, then closed it again, unable to think of anything to say.

In the far corner of the room, a baby monkey started to cry.

ARTHUR C. CLARKE

Catch That Martian

The first person who got on the Martian's nerves, according to a survey I made just recently, was a Mrs Frances Economy, about 42, five foot three, heavy-set, with prominent mole on left cheek, formerly of 302 West 46th Street, Manhattan. Mrs Economy went to a neighbourhood movie on the night of September 5th, and half-way through the first feature, just as she was scrabbling for the last of her popcorn, zip—she wasn't there any more.

That is, she was only half there. She could still see the screen, but it was like a television set with the sound off. The way she realised something had happened to her, she started stomping her feet, like you do when the sound goes off or the picture stops, and her feet didn't make any noise.

In fact, she couldn't feel the floor, just some kind of rubbery arms of her chair. They weren't there, as far as her feeling them went.

Everything was dead still. She could hear her own breathing, and the gulp when she swallowed that last mouthful, and her heart beating if she listened close. That was all. When she got up and went out, she didn't step on anybody's feet—and she *tried* to.

Of course I asked her who was sitting next to her when it happened, but she doesn't remember. She didn't notice. It was like that with everybody.

Not to keep you in suspense, the Martian did it. We figured that out later. There still isn't any proof, but it has to be that way. This Martian, the way it figures, looks just like anybody else. He could be the little guy with the derby hat and the sour expression, or the girl with the china-blue eyes, or the old gent with the chin spinach and glasses on a string. Anybody.

But he's a Martian, I don't see what else he *could* be. And being a Martian, he's got this power that people haven't got. If he feels like it, he just looks at you cockeyed, and zip—you're in some other dimension. I don't know what the scientists would call it, the Fourth or Fifth Dimension or what, but I call it the next-door dimension because it seems like it's right next door—you can see into it. In other words, it's a place where other people can see you, but they can't hear you or touch you, unless they're ghosts too, and there's nothing but some kind of cloudy stuff to walk around on. I don't know if that sounds good or what. It stinks. It's just plain dull.

One more thing, he annoys easy. You crunch popcorn in his ear, he doesn't like that. You step on his toe, same thing. Say, 'Hot enough for you?' or slap him on the back when he's got sunburn, serve him a plate of soup with your finger in it—zip.

The way we figured out it's a Martian was that it couldn't be one of us. No human can do a thing like that. Right? So what else could he be but a Martian? It figures. And nobody ever noticed him, so it must be he looks like everybody else. Some humans, they look like everybody else, but not because they want to. He *wants* to, I bet.

The way we know he annoys easy, there were eighteen 'ghosts' wandering around when the public first noticed, which was during the early morning of September 6th. That was about eleven hours after he got Mrs Economy.

Thirteen of them were up at Broadway and 49th, walking through traffic. They went right through the cars. By nine o'clock there were two wrecks on that corner and a busted hydrant gushing water all over. The ghost people walked through the water and didn't get wet.

Three more showed up in front of a big delicatessen near 72nd Street and Amsterdam Avenue, just looking in the window. Every once in a while one of them would reach in through the glass and grab for something, but his hand went through the pastrami and chopped liver, so none of them got anything. That was fine for store windows, but it wasn't so fine for the ghost people.

The other two were sailors. They were out in the harbour, walking on water and thumbing their noses at naval officers aboard the ships that were anchored out there. It was murder on discipline.

The first eight patrolmen who reported all this got told they would be fired if they ever came on duty drunk again. But by ten-thirty it was on the radio, and then WPIX sent a camera crew up, and by the time the afternoon papers came out there were so many people in Times Square that we had to put a cordon around the ghosts and divert traffic.

The delicatessen window up on Amsterdam got busted from the crowd leaning against it, or some guy trying to put his hand through the way the three ghosts did; we never figured out which. There were about sixty tugs, launches and rowboats in the harbour, and three helicopters, trying to get close enough to talk to the sailors.

One thing we know, the Martian must have been in that crowd on Times Square, because between one and one-thirty p.m. seven more ghosts wandered through the barrier and joined the other ones. You could tell they were mad, but of course you couldn't tell what they were saying unless you could read lips.

Then there were some more down by Macy's in the afternoon, and a few in Greenwich Village, and by evening we had lost count. The guesses in the paper that night ran from three hundred to a thousand. It was the *Times* that said three hundred. The cops didn't give out any estimate at all.

The next day, there was just nothing else at all in the papers, or on the radio or TV. Bars did an all-time record business. So did churches.

The Mayor appointed a committee to investigate. The Police Commissioner called out special reserves to handle the mobs. The Governor was understood to say he was thinking about declaring a statewide emergency, but all he

16

got in most papers was half a column among the ads. Later on he denied the whole thing.

Everybody had to be asked what he thought, from Einstein to Martin and Lewis. Some people said mass hysteria, some said the end of the world, some said the Russians.

Winchell was the first one to say in print that it was a Martian. I had the same idea myself, but by the time I got it all worked out I was too late to get the credit.

I was handicapped, because all this time I still hadn't seen one of the ghosts yet. I was on Safe, Loft and Truck —just promoted last spring from a patrolman—and while I was on duty I never got near any of the places where they were congregating. In the evenings, I had to take care of my mother.

But my brain was working, I had this Martian idea, and I kept thinking, thinking, all the time.

I knew better than to mention this to Captain Rifkowicz. All I would have to do was mention to him that I was thinking, and he would say, 'With what, Dunlop, with what?' or something sarcastic like that. As for asking him to get me transferred to Homicide or Missing Persons, where I might get assigned to the ghost case, that was out. Rifkowicz says I should have been kept on a beat long enough for my arches to fall, in order to leave more room on top for brains.

So I was on my own. And that evening, when they started announcing the rewards, I knew I had to get that Martian. There were fifteen hundred dollars, voted by the City Council that afternoon, for whoever would find out what was making the ghosts and stop it. Because if it didn't stop, there would be eighteen thousand ghosts in a month, and over two hundred thousand in a year.

Then there was a bunch of private rewards, running from twenty-five bucks to five hundred, offered by people that had relatives among the departed. There was a catch to those, though—you had to get the relatives back.

17

All together, they added up to nearly five thousand. With that dough, I could afford to hire somebody to take care of Ma and maybe have some private life of my own. There was a cute waitress down on Varick Street, where I had lunch every day. For a long time I had been thinking if I asked her to go out, maybe she would say yes. But what was the use of me asking her, if all I could do was have her over to listen to Ma talk? All Ma talked about was how sick she was and how nobody cared.

First thing I did, I got together all the newspaper stuff about the ghosts. I spread it out on the living-room table and sorted it and started pasting it into a scrapbook. Right away I saw I had to have more information. What was in the papers was mostly stories about the crowds and the accidents and traffic tie-ups, plus interviews with people that didn't know anything.

What I wanted to know was—what were all these people doing when the Martian got them? If I knew that, maybe I could figure out some kind of pattern, like if the Martian's pet peeve was back-slappers, or people who make you jump a foot when they sneeze, or whatever.

Another thing, I wanted to know all the times and places. From that, I could figure out what the Martian's habits were, if he had any, and with all of it together I could maybe arrange to be put on the spot whenever he got sore. Then anybody except me who was there every time would have to be him.

I explained all this to Ma, hoping she would make a sacrifice and let me get Mrs Proctor from across the hall to sit with her a few evenings. She didn't seem to get the idea. Ma never believes anything she reads in the papers, anyway, except the astrology column. The way it struck her, the whole thing was some kind of a scheme, like gangsters or publicity, and I would be better to stay away from it.

I made one more try, talking up the money I would get, but all she said was, 'Well, then why don't you just *tell* that
18

Captain Rifkowicz he's got to let you earn that reward?'

Ma has funny ideas about a lot of things. She came over here from England when she was a girl, and it looks like she never did get to understand America. I knew that if I kept after her, she would start crying and telling me about all the things she did for me when I was a baby. You can't argue against that.

So what I did next, I took the bull by the horns. I waited till Ma went to sleep and then I just walked out and hopped an uptown bus on Seventh Avenue. If I couldn't get off during the daytime, I would cut down my sleep for a while, that was all.

I was heading for Times Square, but at Twenty-seventh I saw a crowd on the sidewalk. I got out and ran over there. Sure enough, in the middle of the crowd were two of the ghosts, a fat man with a soupstrainer moustache and a skinny woman with cherries on her hat. You could tell they were ghosts because the people were waving their hands through them. Aside from that, there was no difference.

I took the lady first, to be polite. I flashed the badge, and then I hauled out my notebook and wrote, 'Name and address please,' and shoved it at her.

She got the idea and looked through her bag for a pencil and an envelope. She scribbled, 'Mrs Walter F. Walters, Schenectady, N.Y.'

I asked her, 'When did this happen to you and where?'

She wrote it was about one p.m. the afternoon before, and she was in Schrafft's on Broadway near 37th, eating her lunch with her husband, and I asked her if the fat man was her husband, and she said he was.

I then asked her if she could remember exactly what the two of them were doing right at the moment it happened. She thought a while and then said she was talking and her husband was dunking his doughnut in his coffee. I asked her if it was the kind with powdered sugar and she said yes.

I knew then that I was on the right track. She was one of those little women with big jaws that generally seem to

19

have loud voices and like to use them; and I always hated people who dunk those kind of doughnuts, myself. The powdered sugar gets wet and gluey and the dunkers have to lick their fingers right in public.

I thanked them and went on uptown. When I got back home that night, about four a.m. the next morning, I had fifteen interviews in my book. The incidents had taken place all over the mid-town area. Six got theirs for talking, four on crowded sidewalks—probably for jostling or stepping on corns—two for yelling on a quiet street at two in the morning, one for dunking, one for singing to himself on a subway, one, judging by the look of him, for not being washed, and one for coming in late to a Broadway play. The six talkers broke down to three in restaurants, two in a newsreel movie, and one in Carnegie Hall while a concert was going on.

Nobody remembered who they were next to at the time, but I was greatly encouraged. I had a hunch I was getting somewhere already.

I got through the next day, the eighth, in a kind of daze, and don't think Rifkowicz didn't call my attention to it. I suppose I wasn't worth more than a nickel to the City that day, but I promised myself I would make it up later. For the moment, I ignored Rifkowicz.

On the radio and TV, there were two new developments. In my head there was one.

First, the radio and TV. I ate lunch in a saloon so as to catch the latest news, even though I had to give up my daily glimpse of the waitress in the beanery. Two things were new. One, people had started noticing that a few things had turned into ghosts—besides people, I mean. Things like a barrel organ, and an automobile that had its horn stuck, and like that.

That made things twice as bad, of course, because anybody was liable to try to touch one of these ghost things and jump to the conclusion they were a ghost, themselves.

Two, the TV reporters were interviewing the ghosts, the same way I did, with paper and pencil. I picked up four more sets of questions and answers just while I was eating lunch.

The ghosts came over fine on TV, by the way. Somehow it looked even creepier on the screen, when you saw somebody's hand disappear into them, than it did when you saw it with your own eyes.

The development in my head was like this. Out of the fifteen cases I already had, and the four I got from TV, there were eight that happened on the street or in subways or buses, five in restaurants, and six in places of entertainment. Now, at first glance, that may not look like it means much. But I said to myself, 'What does this Martian do? He travels around from one place to another—that's normal. He eats—that's normal. But he goes to four different shows that I know about in three days—and I know just nineteen cases out of maybe a thousand!'

It all fitted together. Here is this Martian. He's never been here before. We know that because he just now started making trouble. The way I see it, these Martians look us over for a while from a distance, and then they decide to send one Martian down to New York to study us close up. Well, what's the first thing he does, being that he wants to find out all about us? He goes to the movies. And concerts, and stage plays too, of course, because he wants to try everything once. But probably he sees two or three double features a day. It stands to reason.

So there he is in the movie, watching and listening so he shouldn't miss anything important, and some customer around him starts making loud comments to somebody else, rattling cellophane, and snapping a pocketbook open and shut every five seconds to find a kleenex. So he flips them into the next dimension, where they can make all the noise they want without bothering him.

And that's the reason why there are so many ghosts that got theirs in the movies and places like that. On the streets of any city you can walk for miles without running into more than two or three really obnoxious characters, but in any kind of theatre there's *always* somebody talking, or coughing, or rattling paper. You've noticed that.

I went even further than that. I checked with my notes and then looked in a copy of *Cue* magazine to find out what was playing at each of those theatres when the Martian was there.

I found out that the play was a long-run musical—the concert was musical, naturally—and one of the two movies was a Hollywood remake of a musical comedy. The other was a newsreel.

There it was. I as good as had him. Then I got another idea and went back through my notes to find out where the theatre victims had been sitting. The guy in Carnegie Hall had been in the balcony; that's where you hear best, I guess. But the other five had all been sitting down front, in the first four rows.

The little guy was nearsighted.

That's the way I was thinking about him now—a little nearsighted guy who liked music better than Westerns, and was used to some place where everybody's careful not to bother anybody else. It was hard not to feel sorry for him; after all, some people that come from places closer than Mars have a hard time in New York.

But it was me against him. That night the total rewards were up to almost twenty thousand dollars.

I thought of one thing I could do right away. I could write to the Mayor to make an announcement that if people didn't want to be ghosts, they should keep from making unnecessary noise or being pests, especially in theatres. But one, he probably wouldn't pay any attention to me, and two, if he did, twenty thousand other guys would be following my lead before I could turn around, and one of them would probably catch the Martian before I did.

That night, I did the same as before. I waited till Ma was

sleeping, then went out to a movie on Broadway. It was a first-run house, they had a musical playing, and I sat down front.

But nothing happened. The Martian wasn't there.

I felt pretty discouraged when I got home. My time was running out and there are over three hundred theatres in Manhattan. I had to start working faster.

I lay awake for a long while, worrying and thinking about it, and finally I came to one of the most important decisions in my life. The next morning I was going to do something I never did before—call in and pretend like I was sick. And I was going to stay sick until I found the Martian.

I felt bad about it and I felt even worse in the morning, when Rifkowicz told me to take it easy till I got well.

After breakfast, I got the papers and made a list of shows on my way uptown. I went to one on 42nd Street first—it was a musical picture about some composer named Handel, and the second feature was a comedy, but it had Hoagy Carmichael in it, so I figured I should stay for that too. I sat in the fifth row. There was plenty of coughing going on, only nobody got turned into a ghost.

Then I had lunch and went to another musical, on Broadway. I drew another blank.

My eyes were beginning to bother me a little from sitting so close to the screen, so I thought I would just go to a newsreel movie and then walk around a while before dinner. But when I got out of the newsreel I began to feel jittery, and I went straight to another double feature. The Martian wasn't there, either.

I had seen plenty of ghosts standing around on the streets, but they were all just standing there looking kind of lost and bewildered, the way they did after a while. You could tell a new victim because he would be rushing here and there, shoving his hands through things, trying to talk to people, and acting all upset.

23

One thing I forgot to mention. Everybody was wondering now how these ghosts got along without eating. In this dimension where they were, there wasn't *anything*, just the stuff like rubbery clouds that they were standing on. But they all claimed they weren't hungry or thirsty, and they all seemed to be in good shape. Even the ones that had been ghosts now for four days.

When I got out of that last movie, it was about eight in the evening. I was feeling low in my mind, but I still had a healthy appetite. I started wandering around the side streets of Broadway, looking for a restaurant that wasn't too crowded or too expensive. I passed a theatre that was on my list, except I knew I was too late to get a ticket for it. It was the premiere of the newest Rodgers and Hammerstein show, and the lobby and half the sidewalk were full of customers.

I went on past, feeling gloomier because of all the bright lights and excitement, and then I heard something funny. Without paying any attention, I had been listening to one of those raspy-voiced barkers inside the lobby going, 'GETcha programme here.' Now all of a sudden, he said 'GETch—' and stopped.

I turned around, with a funny prickling up the back of my spine. The voice didn't start up again. Just as I started back towards the lobby, a ghost came out of the crowd. There was no doubt about him being a ghost—he ran through the people.

He had a bunch of big booklets with slick covers under his arm, and his mouth was wide open like he was shouting. Then he showed his teeth, and his face got all red, and he lifted the booklets in both hands and threw them away as hard as he could. *They* went through people, too.

The ghost walked away with his hands shoved into his pockets.

Running into that lobby, I shoved my badge at the ticket taker, and told him to find me the manager, quick.

When the manager came up I grabbed him by the lapels and said, 'I got reason to believe there's a dangerous criminal going to be in this audience tonight. With your co-operation, we'll get him.' He looked worried, so I said, 'There won't be any trouble. You just put me where I can see the front rows and leave the rest to me.'

He said, 'I can't give you a seat. The house is completely sold out.'

I told him, 'Okay, put me back in the wings, or whatever you call them.'

He argued, but he did what I asked. We went down the side aisle, through the orchestra pit and through a little door that went under the stage. Then we went up a little stairway to backstage, and he put me right at the edge of the stage, up front, where I could peek out at the audience.

There was a crowd of people running around back there behind the curtains, actors and chorus girls, guys in their shirt sleeves and guys in overalls. I could hear the hum out front—people were beginning to fill the seats—and I wanted that curtain to go up. I just couldn't wait.

Finally the actors took their places, and the band suddenly started playing, and the curtain went up.

I understand that show is still playing to standing room only, even with all the trouble that's happened since then, but I didn't pay any attention to it, and I couldn't even tell you what it was about. I was watching the front four rows, trying to memorise every face I saw.

Right in the middle there were three that I paid more attention to than the rest. One of them was a young blonde girl with blue eyes like the colour of Ma's fancy china that she brought with her from the old country. Another was an old gent with a chin spinach and glasses on a string. The third was a little guy with a sour expression and a derby hat.

I don't know why I picked out those three, except maybe it was a hunch. Maybe I was looking at the blonde girl just because she was pretty, but then again, I never saw eyes

25

that colour before or since. It could be that Martians have china-blue eyes; how would I know? I might have had some wild idea that the old guy could be the Martian and was wearing the frizzy white whiskers because Martians don't have chins exactly like us. And I think I picked on the little guy because he fitted the picture I already had in my head. And the way he was clutching that derby in his lap, like it was made of gold—I was thinking to myself, maybe he's got some kind of ray gun built into that hat; maybe that's how he does it.

I admit that I wasn't thinking very logical—I was too excited—but I never took my eyes off that audience for a second.

I was waiting for somebody to start coughing or sneezing and get turned into a ghost. When that happened, I would be watching the people, and if I was lucky I might see who was looking at the victim when it happened.

That's what I was waiting for. What I got was a sniff of smoke and then somebody started screaming and yelling, *'Fire!'*

Half the audience was on their feet in a second. I looked up, and sure enough there was smoke pouring out at the back of the room. Some more women screamed and the stampede was on.

The girls on stage stopped dancing and the band stopped playing. Somebody—some actor—ran out on the stage and started saying, 'Ladies and gentlemen, your attention please. *Walk*, do not run, to the nearest exit. There is no danger. *Walk*, do not run—'

I lost my head. Not on account of the fire. I knew the actor was right and the only bad thing that could happen would be people trampling each other to death to get out of there. But the seats were emptying fast and it struck me all of a sudden that I didn't know my way through that tangle of scenery backstage. By the time I got down the stairs and out into the auditorium, the Martian might be gone.

I felt cold all over. I didn't even stop to remember that I didn't have to go back the way I came, because there were little steps right at the side of the stage. I ran out from behind the wings and started to jump over the musicians. At that, I would have made it if I hadn't caught my toe in that little trough where the footlights are.

I had worse luck than that, even. I landed smack in the middle of the bass drum.

You never heard such a noise in your life. It sounded as if the ceiling caved in. Sitting there, with my legs and arms sticking out of that drum, I saw the people turn around and look at me like they had been shot. I saw them all, the girl with the china-blue eyes, the old gent with the whiskers, the little guy with the derby, and a lot more. And then, suddenly, all the sound stopped, same as when you turn off a radio.

The guy who owned the drum leaned over and tried to pull me out of it. He couldn't.

His hands went right through me.

Like I said, this Martian annoys easy. I don't know what he did about all those women screaming—maybe he figured there was a good reason for that and left them alone. But when I hit that bass drum, it must have burned him good. You know, when you're excited already, a loud noise will make you jump twice as far.

That's about the only satisfaction I got—that I probably annoyed him the worst of anybody in New York City.

That and being so close to catching him.

The company here is nothing to brag about—women that will talk your arm off and half your shoulder, and guys that say, 'Peaceful enough for you?' and back-slappers, and people that hum to themselves—

Besides that, the place is so damned dull. Clouds to stand on, nothing to eat even if you wanted to eat, and nothing

27

to do except stand around and watch the new ones come through. We can't see much of New York any more, because it keeps getting mistier all the time—fading away, kind of, like maybe this dimension is getting a little farther away from the ordinary one every day.

I asked Mr Dauth yesterday how he thought the whole thing would wind up. Mr Dauth isn't bad. He's a big, cheerful guy, about fifty. The kind that likes good food and good beer and a lot of it. But he doesn't complain. He admits that his habit of sucking his teeth out real loud is aggravating and says maybe he deserved what he got, which you'll admit is big of him. So I talk to him a lot, and the other day, when we were watching a new batch that had just come through, I asked him where he thought it would all end, because we can hear each other, you see, being in the same dimension.

He pursed his lips and frowned like he was thinking it over, and then said that as far as he could see, there wasn't any human being that was perfect. Anybody is liable to do something aggravating sooner or later. That's the way people are.

'And this Martian of yours seems to be thorough,' he said. 'Very thorough. It might take him years to get through studying the Earth.'

'And then what?' I asked him.

'Well,' he said, 'eventually, if he keeps it up long enough, we'll *all* be over here.'

I hope he's right. Now that I come to think of it, that cute waitress I mentioned has a habit of setting down a coffee cup so half of it slops into the saucer. If Mr Dauth is right, all I've got to do is wait.

It stands to reason.

DAMON KNIGHT

The Wind

The phone rang at six thirty that evening. It was December, and already dark as Thompson picked up the phone.

'Hello.'

'Hello, *Herb?*'

'Oh, it's you, Allin.'

'Is your wife at home, Herb?'

'Sure. Why?'

'Damn it.'

Herb Thompson spoke into the receiver quietly. 'What's up? You sound funny.'

'I wanted you to come over tonight.'

'We're having company.'

'I wanted you to spend the night. When's your wife going away?'

'That's next week,' said Thompson. 'She'll be in Ohio for about nine days. Her mother's sick. I'll come over then.'

'I wish you could come over tonight.'

'Wish I could. Company and all, my wife'd kill me.'

'I wish you could come over.'

'What is it? The wind again?'

'Oh, no. No.'

'Is it the wind?' asked Thompson.

The voice on the phone hesitated. 'Yeah. Yeah, it's the wind.'

'It's a clear night, there's not much wind.'

'There's enough. It comes in the window and blows the curtains a little bit. Just enough to tell me.'

'Look, why don't you come and spend the night here?' said Herb Thompson looking around the lighted hall.

'Oh, no. It's too late for that. It might catch me on the

29

way over. It's a damned long distance, I wouldn't dare, but thanks, anyway. It's thirty miles, but thanks.'

'Take a sleeping tablet.'

'I've beeen standing in the door for the past hour, Herb. I can see it building up in the west. There are some clouds there and I saw one of them kind of rip apart. There's a wind coming, all right.'

'Well, you just take a nice sleeping tablet. And call me any time you want to call. Later this evening if you want.'

'Any time?' said the voice on the phone.

'Sure.'

'I'll do that, but I wish you could come out. Yet I wouldn't want you hurt. You're my best friend and I wouldn't want that. Maybe it's best to face this thing alone. I'm sorry I bother you.'

'Hell, what's a friend for? Tell you what to do, sit down and get some writing done this evening,' said Herb Thompson, shifting from one foot to the other in the hall. 'You'll forget about the Himalayas and the Valley of the Winds and this preoccupation of yours with storms and hurricanes. Get another chapter done on your next travel book.'

'I might do that. Maybe I will, I don't know. Maybe I will. I might do that. Thanks a lot for letting me bother you.'

'Thanks, hell! Get off the line now, you. My wife's calling me to dinner.'

Herb Thompson hung up.

He went and sat down at the supper table and his wife sat across from him. 'Was that Allin?' she asked. He nodded. 'Him and his winds that blow up and winds that blow down and winds that blow hot and blow cold,' she said, handing him his plate heaped with food.

'He did have a time in the Himalayas, during the war,' said Herb Thompson.

'You don't believe what he said about that valley, do you?'

'It makes a good story.'

30

'Climbing around, climbing up things. Why do men climb mountains and scare themselves?'

'It was snowing,' said Herb Thompson.

'Was it?'

'And raining and hailing and blowing all at once, in that valley. Allin's told me a dozen times. He tells it well. He was up pretty high. Clouds, and all. The valley made a noise.'

'I *bet* it did,' she said, sulkily.

'Like a lot of winds instead of just one. Winds from all over the world.' He took a bite. 'So says Allin.'

'He shouldn't have gone there and looked, in the first place,' she said. 'You go poking around and first thing you know you get ideas. Winds start getting angry at you for intruding, and they follow you.'

'Don't joke at him, he's my best friend,' snapped Herb Thompson.

'It's all so silly!'

'Nevertheless, he's been through a lot. That storm in Bombay, later, and the hurricane in the Pacific islands two months after that. And that time in Cornwall.'

'I have no sympathy for a man who continually runs into wind storms and hurricanes, and then gets a persecution complex because of it.'

The phone rang again.

'Don't answer it,' she said.

'Maybe it's important.'

'It's only Allin, again.'

They sat there and the phone rang nine times and they didn't answer. Finally, it quieted. They finished dinner. Out in the kitchen, the curtains gently moved in a small breeze from a slightly opened window.

The phone rang again.

'I can't let it ring,' he said, and answered it. 'Oh, hello, Allin.'

'Herb! It's here! It got here!'

'You're too near the phone, back away a little.'

31

'I stood in the open door and waited for it. I saw it coming down the highway, shaking all the treees, one by one, until it shook the trees just outside the house and it dived down towards the door and I slammed the door in its face!'

Thompson didn't say anything. He couldn't think of anything to say, his wife was watching him in the hall door.

'How interesting,' he said, at last.

'It's all around the house, Herb. I can't get out now, I can't do anything. But I fooled it, I let it think it had me, and just as it came down to get me I slammed and locked the door! I was ready for it, I've been getting ready for weeks.'

'Have you, now; tell me about it, Allin, old man,' Herb Thompson said jovially into the phone, while his wife looked on and his neck began to sweat.

'It began six weeks ago . . .'

'Oh, yes? Well, well.'

'. . . I thought I had it licked. I thought it had given up following and trying to get me. But it was just waiting. Six weeks ago I heard the wind laughing and whispering around the corners of my house, out here. Just for an hour or so, not very long, not very loud. Then it went away.'

Thompson nodded into the phone. 'Glad to hear it, glad to hear it.' His wife stared at him.

'It came back, the next night. It slammed the shutters and kicked sparks out of the chimney. It came back five nights in a row, a little stronger each time. When I opened the front door, it came in at me and tried to pull me out, but it wasn't strong enough. Tonight it *is*.'

'Glad to hear you're feeling better,' said Thompson.

'I'm not better, what's wrong with you? Is your wife listening to us?'

'Yes.'

'Oh, I see. I know I sound like a fool.'

'Not at all. Go on.'

Thompson's wife went back into the kitchen. He relaxed. He sat down on a little chair near the phone. 'Go on, Allin, get it out of you, you'll sleep better.'

'It's all around the house now, like a great big vacuum machine nuzzling at all the gables. It's knocking the trees around.'

'That's funny, there's no wind *here*, Allin.'

'Of course not, it doesn't care about you, only about me!'

'I guess that's one way to explain it.'

'It's a killer, Herb, the biggest damnedest prehistoric killer that ever hunted prey. A big sniffling hound, trying to smell me out, find me. It pushes its big cold nose up to the house, taking air, and when it finds me in the parlour it drives its pressure there, and when I'm in the kitchen it goes there. It's trying to get in the windows, now, but I had them reinforced and I put new hinges on the doors, and bolts. It's a strong house. They built them strong in the old days. I've got all the lights in the house on, now. The house is all lit up, bright. The wind followed me from room to room, looking through all the windows, when I switched them on. Oh!'

'What's wrong?'

'It just snatched off the verandah door!'

'I wish you'd come over here and spend the night, Allin.'

'I can't! God, I can't leave the house. I can't do anything. I know this wind, Lord, it's big and it's smart. I tried to light a cigarette a moment ago, and a little draught sucked the match out. The wind likes to play games, it likes to taunt me, it's taking its time with me, it's got all night. And now! God, right now, one of my old travel books, on the library table, I wish you could see it. A little breeze from God knows what small hole in the house has flipped the cover of the book open and the little breeze is —turning the pages one by one. I wish you could see it. There's my introduction. Do you remember the introduction to my Tibet book, Herb?'

'Yes.'

'This book is dedicated to those who lost the game of elements, written by one who has seen, but who has always escaped.'

'Yes, I remember.'

'The lights have gone out!'

The phone crackled.

'The power lines just went down. Are you there, Herb?'

'I still hear you.'

'The wind got jealous of all that light in my house, it tore the power lines down. The telephone will probably go next. Oh, it's a real party, me and the wind, I tell you! Just a second.'

'Allin?' A silence. Herb leaned against the mouthpiece. His wife glanced in from the kitchen. Herb Thompson waited. 'Allin?'

'I'm back,' said the voice on the phone. 'There was a draught from the door and I shoved some wadding under it to keep it from cooling my legs. I'm glad you didn't come out after all, Herb, I wouldn't want you in this mess. It just broke one of the living room windows and a regular gale is in the house, knocking pictures off the wall. Do you hear it?'

Herb Thompson listened. There was a wild sirening on the phone and a whistling and banging. Allin shouted over it. 'Do you hear it?'

Herb Thompson swallowed drily. 'I hear it.'

'It wants me alive, Herb. It doesn't dare knock the house down in one fell blow. That'd kill me. It wants me alive, so it can pull me apart, finger by finger. It wants what's inside me. My mind, my brain. It wants my life-power, my psychic force, my ego. It wants intellect.'

'My wife's calling me, Allin, I have to go and dry the dishes.'

'It's a big cloud of vapours, winds from all over the world. The same wind that ripped the Celebes a year ago, the same pampero that killed in Argentina, the typhoon that fed well in Hawaii, and the hurricane that knocked
34

the coast of Africa early this year. It's part of all those storms I escaped. It followed me from the Himalayas because it didn't want me to know what I know of it, the Valley of the Winds where it gathers and plans its destruction. Something, a long time ago, gave it a start in the direction of life. I know its feeding grounds, I know where it is born and where parts of it expire. For that reason, it hates me, for I have written books against it, telling how to defeat it. It doesn't want me preaching any more. It wants to incorporate me into its huge body, give it knowledge. It wants me on its own side!'

'I have to hang up, Allin, my wife—'

'What?' A pause, the blowing of the wind in the phone, distantly. 'What did you say?'

'Call me back in about an hour, Allin.'

He hung up.

He went out to dry the dishes. His wife looked at him and he looked at the dishes, rubbing them with a towel.

'What's it like out tonight?' he said.

'Nice. Not very chilly. Stars,' she said. 'Why?'

'Nothing.'

The phone rang three times in the next hour. At eight o'clock the company arrived, Stoddard and his wife. They sat around until eight-thirty talking and then got out and set up the card table and began to play.

Herb Thompson shuffled the cards over and over, with a clittering, shuttering effect and clapped them out, one at a time before the three other players. Talk went back and forth. He lit a cigar and made it into a fine grey ash at the tip, and adjusted his cards in his hand and on occasion lifted his head and listened. There was no sound outside the house. His wife saw him do this, and he cut it out immediately, and discarded a Jack of Clubs.

He puffed slowly on his cigar and they all talked quietly with occasionally small eruptions of laughter, and the clock in the hall sweetly chimed nine o'clock.

'Here we all are,' said Herb Thompson, taking his cigar out and looking at it reflectively. 'And life is sure funny.'

'Eh?' said Mr Stoddard.

'Nothing, except here we are, living our lives, and somewhere else on earth a billion other people live their lives.'

'That's a rather naïve statement.'

'True, nevertheless. Life,' he put his cigar back in his lips, 'is a lonely thing. Even with married people. Sometimes when you're in a person's arms you feel a million miles away from them.'

'I like *that*,' said his wife.

'I didn't mean it that way,' he explained, not with haste; because he felt no guilt, he took his time. 'I mean we all believe what we believe and live our own little lives while other people live entirely different ones. I mean, we sit here in this room while a thousand people are dying. Some of cancer, some of pneumonia, some of tuberculosis. I imagine someone in the United States is dying right now in a motor crash.'

'This isn't very stimulating conversation,' said his wife.

'I mean to say, we all live and don't think about how other people think or live their lives or die. We wait until death comes *to* us. What I mean is here we sit, on our self-assured butt-bones, while, thirty miles away, in a big old house, completely surrounded by night and God-knows-what, one of the finest guys who ever lived is—'

'Herb!'

He puffed and chewed on his cigar and stared blindly at his cards. 'Sorry.' He blinked rapidly and bit his cigar. 'Is it my turn?'

'It's your turn.'

The play went round the table, with a fluttering of cards, murmurs, conversation, laughter. Herb Thompson sank lower into his chair and began to look ill.

The phone rang. Thompson jumped and ran to it and jerked it off the hook.

'Herb! I've been calling and calling.'

'I couldn't answer, my wife wouldn't let me.'

'What's it like at your house, Herb?'

'What do you mean, what's it like?'

'Has the company come?'

'Hell, yes, it has—'

'Are you talking and laughing and playing cards?'

'Damn it, yes, but what has that got to do with—'

'Are you smoking your ten-cent cigar?'

'Yes, but . . .'

'Swell,' said the voice on the phone, enviously. 'That sure is swell. I wish I could be there. I wish I didn't know the things I know. I wish lots of things.'

'Are you all right?'

'So far, so good. I'm locked in the kitchen now. The front wall of the house just blew in. But I've planned my retreat. When the kitchen door gives, I'm heading for the cellar. If I'm lucky I may hold out there until morning. It'll have to tear the whole damned house down to get to me, and the cellar floor is pretty solid. I have a shovel and I may dig —deeper . . .'

It sounded like a lot of other voices on the phone.

'What's *that?*' Herb Thompson demanded, cold, shivering.

'That?' asked the voice on the phone. 'Those are the voices of ten thousand killed in a typhoon, seven thousand killed by a hurricane, three thousand buried by a cyclone. Am I boring you? It's a long list. That's what the wind is, you know. It's a lot of spirits, a lot of people dead. The wind killed them and took their intellects, their spirits, to give itself intelligence. It took all their voices and made them into one voice. Interesting, isn't it? All those millions of peoples killed in the past centuries, twisted and tortured and taken from continent to continent on the backs and in the bellies of monsoons and whirlwinds. I get very poetic at a time like this.'

The phone echoed and rang with voices and shouts and whinings.

'Come on back, Herb,' said his wife, at the card table.

'That's how the wind gets more intelligent each year, it adds to its intellect, body by body, life by life, death by death.'

'We're waiting for you, Herb,' called his wife.

'Damn it!' he turned, almost snarling. 'Wait just a moment, won't you!' Back to the phone. 'Allin, if you want me to come out there now, I will, if you need help.'

'Wouldn't think of it. This is a grudge fight, wouldn't do to have you in it. Well, I'd better hang up. The kitchen door looks very weak and I'll have to get into the cellar.'

'Call me back, later?'

'Maybe, if I'm lucky. I don't think I'll make it this time. I slipped away and escaped in the Celebes that time, but I think it has me now. I hope I haven't bothered you too much, Herb.'

'You haven't bothered anyone, damn it. Call me back.'

'I'll try...'

Herb Thompson went back to the card game. His wife glared at him. 'How's Allin, your friend?' she asked. 'Is he sober?'

'He's never taken a drink in his life,' said Thompson sullenly, sitting down. 'I should have gone out there earlier.'

'But he's called every night for six weeks and you've been out there least ten nights to sleep with him and everything was all right.'

'He needs help. He might hurt himself.'

'You were out there two nights ago, you can't always be running after him.'

'First thing in the morning I'll move him into a nursing home. Didn't want to. He seems so reasonable, so sane.'

They played out the games. At ten-thirty coffee was served. Herb Thompson drank his slowly, looking at the phone. I wonder if he's in the cellar now, he thought.

Herb Thompson walked to the phone, called long-distance, put through a call.

38

'I'm sorry,' said the operator. 'The lines are down in that district. As soon as the lines have been repaired, we will put your call through.'

'Then the telephone lines *are* down!' cried Thompson, slamming down the phone. Turning, he ran down the hall, opened the cupboard, pulled out his hat and coat. 'Excuse me,' he shouted. 'You *will* excuse me, won't you? I'm sorry,' he said, to his amazed guests and his wife with the coffee urn in her hand.

'Herb!' she cried. 'I've got to get out there!' he said, in return.

He slipped into his coat.

There was a soft, faint stirring at the door.

Everybody in the room tensed and straightened up.

'Who could that be?' asked his wife.

The soft stirring was repeated, very quietly.

Thompson hurried down the hall where he stopped, alert.

Outside, faintly, he heard laughter.

'I'll be damned,' said Thompson. He put his hand on the door-knob, pleasantly shocked and relieved. 'I'd know that laugh anywhere. It's Allin. He came on over in his car, after all. Couldn't wait until morning to tell me his confounded tall tales.' Thompson chuckled weakly. 'Probably brought some friends with him. Sounds like a lot of other people . . .'

He opened the front door.

The verandah was empty.

Thompson showed no surprise, his face grew amusedly sly. He laughed. 'Allin? None of your tricks now! Come on.' He switched on the verandah light and peered out and around. 'Where are you, Allin? Come on, now.'

A little breeze blew into his face.

Thompson waited a moment, suddenly chilled to his marrow. He stepped out of the door and looked uneasily about, very carefully.

A sudden wind caught and whipped his coat flaps, dishevelled his hair.

He thought he heard laughter again. The wind suddenly rounded the house and was a pressure everywhere at once, and then, storming for a full minute, passed on.

The wind died down, sad, mourning in the high trees, passing away; going back out to the sea, to the Celebes, to the Ivory Coast, to Sumatra and Cape Horn, to Cornwall and the Philippines. Fading, fading, fading.

Thompson stood there, cold. He went in and closed the door and leaned against it, and didn't move, eyes closed.

'What's wrong . . .?' asked his wife.

RAY BRADBURY

Small Lords

Cliteman picked his way mincingly along the greenish sands of the beach. It was nearly dark, and that made it bad, because he had to watch where he was stepping. The crazy young ones were just as likely as not to run across his path for a thrill. And if he missed seeing one in the dusk, and stepped on it ...

He swallowed and moved closer to the water's edge. It might be best, everything considered, to swim back; but he didn't like the thought of that brackish water in the sores on his back. The foreman had given him an unusually hard time that day—well, maybe the foreman's wife had given *him* a hard time that morning and he was just taking it out on Cliteman. If the foreman had a wife.

Cliteman stopped at the outskirts of the little village he called Salt Lake City and whistled, as he had learned it was best to do. The greenish, jewel-like lights in the windows of the tiny houses were all on; and the larger, bluer lights in the streets gave Cliteman a pretty good view, even though the light from setting Canopus was rapidly dwindling.

Cliteman saw that one of the midges was waving at him, and he squatted down. The midge was big for its race, very nearly half an inch tall. It stood on two legs like a man; it had two arms like a man, and a head like a man's head. The glossy eyes that covered nearly the whole head were not a man's, of course, and the shrill, piping voice was closer to the stridulations of an insect.

It was waving him away from the village off the beach. Cliteman saw why; there was some sort of gathering on the sands, several hundred of the midges. Without resentment, he waded into the shallows and around the town, though the sting of the water on his scarred legs was extremely painful.

But that wasn't important to Cliteman at the moment. What was important was that he was almost unbearably hungry. If only Morris had found something decent to eat for a change! A couple of dozen of the big pink shellfish perhaps, or one of those big, six-legged swimming things that tasted faintly of peach-pits . . .

Splat. Cliteman yelled involuntarily as the biting greenish spark charred a tiny crater in his shoulder. One of the midges was standing threateningly on a rock in his path aiming at him with the glistening small hand weapons that they used for disciplining the earthmen—or for killing each other as the occasion arose.

Splat. Another spark flared close by, this one only a warning. Cliteman clutched his shoulder and, ever so gently, moved farther out into the water. It was important not to move quickly; the spray a fast-moving foot might kick up was enough to drown a midge.

And that was about all he needed. If he killed one of them, that would be the end of everything. Cliteman vividly remembered what had happened to Fuller when he had crushed one of the little aliens. Quite by accident; but the aliens either didn't know that, or didn't care.

It wasn't that they were deliberately cruel in the way they destroyed Fuller; or at least, Cliteman thought it wasn't. But these beings were tiny and humans huge; they had only tiny weapons against the gross flesh monoliths from the exploring ship. Death at the hands of the midges was like death from an army of raging termites. It came with a hundred, a thousand, ten thousand little, painful, finally fatal wounds. Perhaps there weren't any good ways to die, Cliteman thought, but certainly there were few that were worse.

As quickly as he could, Cliteman hurried down the brackish sea's shore, each step a carefully planned, meticulously executed problem in engineering. He tried to stay ankle-deep in the water, away from possible wandering midges on the beach, but not so deep that his steps would splash any who might come by. The foot carefully lifted and carefully brought forward; the toe pointed out just so, slipped into the water ahead as delicately as possible.

Just ahead was the little cape the aliens had indicated the human giants might use for their own, free and clear. 'Morris!' cried Cliteman. 'Hello there!'

No answer; not even the gleam of firelight, where Morris should already have had the fire going, cooking whatever he had been able to turn up in the way of food. Morris was the official provider for the humans, permitted by the tiny aliens to labour only half a day on the crude projects they had assigned the others, so that he might have time to find and prepare the enormous masses of food the giants required. 'Morris! Are you there?'

But he wasn't there. Cliteman was alone.

Canopus was down now, and the only light was from the bluish star they called Neighbour. From Earth, Neighbour was only a tiny spot of light—twelfth magnitude or thereabouts—smaller than the 200-inch telescope. But it happened to hang close in space to the system of Canopus. Though its absolute magnitude was only four or five times the brightness of the Sun, it was close enough so that in the night sky it seemed brighter than Earth's moon, bright enough to see by, uncomfortably bright to look at direct.

There was not, however, light enough to make it easy for Cliteman to tend his nets. After half an hour he hauled in his catch; something throbbed and leaped in the purse. He pulled on the long, precious ropes with his mouth watering; it wasn't until he had the net on the sand, maddeningly empty, that he saw he had neglected to fasten the other end. The prey had escaped; he grimly tied the necessary knots, and cast it out again.

Cliteman lay down on the beach to wait. It was getting chilly—the planet's air was thin. Canopus provided plenty of heat by day, but with the setting of their sun the temperature dropped thirty or forty degrees in as many minutes. The fire was a comfort, but of course it didn't do to make it large—everything on the planet's surface was on a smallish scale; the largest vegetation not much taller than a man. Already in only a few months, they had nearly denuded the little cape that was set aside for them of burnable brush, and there was no way of knowing if the midges would permit them to extend their foraging inland. The trouble was, they couldn't talk to the midges. It was not merely a matter of language, but the auditory range of the little aliens was pitched bat-high; only the sharpest whistles of the earthmen could be heard by the midges—as bass rumbles, no doubt.

Cliteman stared wearily at Neighbour through half closed eyes. Somewhere about Neighbour, the interstellar ship would be orbiting now, while its scout rockets surveyed the half-dozen planets they had located from space. The ship had been gone six months; it would be gone six months more, at least.

There was a grave doubt in Cliteman's mind that any of them would survive another six months of this.

There had been ten men in the scout rocket that set down on Canopus's sixth planet. Three were dead—Fuller under the weapons of the midges, Breck and Hogarth when the rocket crashed. Morris was sick—it was no charity that made the midges let him have his half-day off; even the tiny aliens could see that the radioman was in bad shape.

And the rest of them were slaves.

Something whistled through the air high overhead—a hundred yards or more. Cliteman instinctively stood up and raised his hand to identify himself. It was a midge flyer, one of the foot-long jets that he had seen from time to time on mysterious errands, no doubt diverted from whatever course it had been pursuing by the sight of his fire. It circled, with a thin noise like a swinging whip, and

44

Cliteman saw the pattern of coloured lights on its dragonfly wings that seemed to be an identification marking. 'Take a good look!' he mumbled to himself. He looked more closely himself, and saw that this particular jet was much smaller than others he had seen. It couldn't have been more than three or four inches long, he guessed, as it spiralled down within a few yards of his head. No doubt a one-'man' ship to be used for—for . . .

Cliteman lowered his hands sourly, craning his neck to stare down the shore where Morris should have been coming, but wasn't. He didn't *know* what the midges might use a one-man jet for. Did they have wars? Perhaps; and perhaps a small jet might be a fighter. But it was only a guess, and the chances were extremely good that any guess any of the earthmen might make about the midges was quite wrong. There had been no chance to learn; the scout rocket had come in without orbiting—though no amount of orbiting would have done much good, since no conceivable midge installation would have been visible from space. They had observed nothing in the descent, beyond the bare outlines of the planet's geography; they had crashed in landing, and had stumbled out into an aroused hornet's nest of mighty little warriors.

And from then on, nothing.

The tiny jet whipped once more around him and shot out over the water. Cliteman touched his sore shoulder with a gentle hand, staring absently after it.

Then he focused his eyes and his attention. Something was floundering in the net.

Dinner! He jumped for the ropes that he and Morris had so painstakingly pieced together and pulled the purse towards shore. Whatever it was that was in the net, it was of a size that promised a full meal! Be damned to Morris, Cliteman thought rebelliously; let him go hungry then! He carefully jockeyed the net into the shallows, and in Neighbour's blue-white light he saw the thrashing sea-creature's struggles break the surface of the water. He played it as any angler plays a trout, fully concentrated, aware of nothing but his net and his prey . . .

Disastrously aware of nothing; for disaster came.

He heard, a little too late, the deeper, slower whistle of the jet again. He looked up a little too late, and saw it settling down towards the water, close inshore, just beyond his net.

The jet's tiny pilot was landing!

Cliteman pulled frantically at the ropes; then dropped them. Too late! The jet seemed to falter and swerve, as though the pilot had at last seen the treacherous snarl of ropes, and the leaping sea-creature in the water before him. Too late. The tiny aircraft had already touched its narrow keel to the water; it bounced on one cord and spun around another; it ploughed into the tangle of the net itself and flipped over.

Cliteman, panicky, leapt knee-deep into the water and clutched at the doll-sized aircraft. He roared and jerked his hands away; stupid of him to have touched the jet exhaust! He grasped it gently around the middle of the fuselage and lifted it, held it in his hand, staring. It was impossible to see the pilot in only the light from Neighbour; in a moment he brought it to the fire and set it down on a little rock, and knelt to peer inside the little transparent hatch.

The pilot was inside, all right; but motionless. Unconscious, perhaps, or dead.

In either case, there was no doubt in Cliteman's mind that he was in trouble.

Morris limped slowly towards the reservation.

He was hungry, in spite of the wearing, burning pain in his chest that had been getting worse ever since the rocket crash; and he was bone-tired. His whole back was a pattern of new scars as well; it had taken quite a few applications of the midges' weapons before he understood that this day was not like all the other days, that this day the midges did not intend to permit him to leave his work half way through the day. The scars were the penalty he had to pay for not understanding; but it didn't make them less painful.

Besides, there would be trouble with Cliteman, Morris knew with resignation. How close to the beast they had all returned! Take the case of Sanford Cliteman, lieutenant in the Space Force, respected citizen, loved husband and father of two. Morris had played many a game of chess with Cliteman on the way out, the lieutenant had been a skilled opponent, generous in victory, good-natured in defeat.

Yet, what about the time three days before when Morris had torn the net and there had been no dinner ready for Cliteman? The man's anger had been animal—and Morris himself had flared into anger in response; the two of them had come close to a fist-fight. Animal!

But how could they help it? They were treated as beasts, mindless prime movers suitable for clearing land for the strange midge farms, or for scrabbling at the earth to make culverts and irrigation ditches. If they offended, they were given a beast's punishment, a touch of the whip. If they served well, they got a beast's reward, to be turned loose at sundown—free to feed and sleep. That was the greatest gift the midges ever gave.

'Why?' Morris demanded, puffing and holding his bad leg as he limped along. It seemed impossible that the midges should not realize they were intelligent, highly civilized beings. They had seen the rocket; they could not imagine beasts could create or man such a machine. But there was simply no sign of an attempt at communication.

In the fury of the first fight, the earthmen had been completely off guard. The rocket had crashed; that put an end to the book's rules about first contact on an alien planet. They had stumbled out of the wreck, mostly unharmed, mostly hurt or shaken up. They had been greeted with fire from the midge hand weapons, and even more serious fire from what might have been the equivalent of self-propelled artillery. Well, maybe they should have reacted quicker,

47

Morris thought; they could have stuck together, leaped back into the rocket in spite of the threat of fire and explosion, armed themselves, fought off the aliens. But in the split second when that was still possible they had wavered.

Carrasquel had drawn his gun and begun return fire; but the equation one bullet—one midge did not balance to the advantage of the earthmen. Undoubtedly Carrasquel had killed a few, but what was the use of killing a few—or a hundred—or a thousand? Fuller hadn't a gun, but he had stamped at them as though they were insects. It was Fuller the midges destroyed, in cold blood, while he lay in helpless anguish under the shock of their concentrated fire. Concentrated, that was it; the midges had leaped into action, each group fixed firmly on a target; the humans in their surprise had blundered and scattered. And they never had really got together again. The midge tactics had evidently been to keep them apart, for the fire was most punishing when any two of the earthmen tried to come together . . .

And now there was Cliteman and himself, who had been driven miles and miles across country, under the stings of the pursuing midges in their vehicles and their aircraft. He knew where Carrasquel and Boehm were, because he'd chanced to see Boehm and they'd been able to shout to each other for a moment; the others he hadn't even seen in months.

But if only the midges had waited—if only the midges had tried to make contact, come to appreciate that earthmen were their superiors, in any imaginable scale of intellectual values . . .

But come to think of it, Morris told himself dourly, that was no longer so very true.

Morris laboured around the little hill that went down to the water and saw Cliteman fiddling with something on the ground. There was no smell of cooking fish; there was something wrong. 'Cliteman, what's the matter?'

The lieutenant jumped up, startled, his eyes wild. Then

he saw who it was. 'Oh, Morris. This damn midge— Where the hell have you been? I've been starving— Never mind that. Look what I've got here!'

Morris looked, and opened his eyes, and looked again. He whispered, 'Sweet love of heaven!'

'What am I going to do?' Cliteman demanded. 'Look at the damn things, Morris. They're hurt! They might be dying, for all I know.'

'They?'

Cliteman said bitterly. 'Three of them; three little midges, out for a little excursion. Momma Midge and Poppa Midge and Little Bitty Baby Midge—I guess. And what do you think they'll make of that, Morris? I've been sitting here trying to make up my mind to chuck them back in the drink.'

'No, Cliteman!'

Cliteman stared at him woodenly for a second. 'Remember Fuller?' he asked after a moment.

'I know, Cliteman, but . . .'

'They'll think *I* killed them! And how do I know? Maybe I did. If I hadn't been pulling in the net just when they landed their stinking plane it would have been all right! But here they are, and do you know what comes next, Morris? Because I don't!'

Morris lowered himself gingerly to the ground—something he was reluctant to do, because it wasn't always easy getting up again. 'Shut up a minute,' he ordered, and looked closely at the midge plane.

There were three of them in it, all right. Two stirring faintly, one motionless. Dead? Morris had no idea. They all had their eyes open, but as far as Morris or Cliteman knew, midges had nothing to close their eyes with; neither of them had ever seen one blink. The transparent canopy was smashed open. Apparently, Cliteman's first frantic idea was to get the three of them out of the plane, but once he'd opened the canopy he hadn't dared touch them.

Morris stared dazedly at the tiny machine. It was a beau-

49

tifully made child's toy; any kid on earth would have given his chance of immortality for one like it. Three inches long, five inches from wingtip to where the other wingtip would have been if it hadn't been crumpled flat. It was still in working condition except for the wings and the canopy— at any rate, tiny red and purple lights winked on what might have been the instrument panel, and something that Morris couldn't see was making a faint, high-pitched hum.

Morris propped himself on an elbow and ventured to touch one of the midges with a delicately questing finger. It moved slightly, but whether it was cold to the touch, or warm he couldn't have said.

He noticed silvery threads and rods, so small they were almost invisible, tangled in a little heap on a flat rock beside the ship. 'What's that?'

Cliteman took a deep breath. He sounded a little more human as he said, 'I don't know. I thought they might be —well, radio antennae or something. I broke them off. Didn't want them calling for help.'

Morris shook his head. Cliteman cried, 'Don't tell me I shouldn't have done that! Maybe I shouldn't have, but— curse it, Morris, I was scared! Don't forget Fuller.'

Morris sighed. He said wearily. 'I'm hungry,' and pushed himself to a sitting position, still looking at the little plane. 'They kept me working till dark,' he said absently. 'I guess they decided I'm well enough to put in a full day's work now. Or maybe that I'm not well enough to be worth pampering—might as well work me to death. I don't suppose you caught anything to eat?'

'Morris, don't you see what trouble we're in?'

Morris looked at Cliteman soberly. 'They'll blame us for sure!' Morris noted that it was 'us' who had become responsible for what had happened to the midge plane. 'Look, Morris, the way I see it there are only two things we can do. One, we can get rid of it—sink it in the ocean, and hope they never find it. Maybe they won't. Maybe they
50

won't connect us with what happened to the plane.'

'And maybe they will,' said Morris.

'All right, they will,' Cliteman agreed. 'Sure, why kid ourselves? So that only leaves one thing. It's time for us to make our break, Morris. Like we talked about. We'll cut straight across country till we find that big river and stay right with it. It can't be more than ten miles. We won't miss the rocket, it's too big. What do you say, Morris? We've been planning to do it anyhow as soon as you were feeling better. Well, this just moves the date up. We can't wait. It's too big a risk, Morris; remember Fuller. What about it? If we ...'

'Shut up.' Cliteman blinked and stared. 'No, *shut up!*' Morris sat straight, peering at the sky. It wasn't anger that had made him tell the lieutenant to shut up, although he felt something that came close to anger.

He had heard something.

He listened; the two of them listened.

They heard it, and then in a moment they saw: the faint whistle, the patterned lights of a midge jet circling overhead.

'Act busy!' cried Cliteman; 'Start putting wood on the fire!'

He himself leaped towards the net, where the neglected fish-thing was feebly flapping away what remained of its strength. He drew it in while Morris laboriously got to his feet and fed the fire. Cliteman grasped the slippery creature, reckless of possible teeth or stinging spines. He bashed it expertly against a rock and then took a closer look at it. It was tentacled, not much over a foot long and plump as a frog's belly. Cliteman quickly skewered it on a gnarled stem of green wood and handed it to Morris to broil.

'But you didn't clean it!' Morris protested. 'We can't eat this without ...'

'Cook it! We aren't going to eat it, you idiot. Just look busy until that damn plane goes away.'

Cliteman glanced warily up. It was still there, perhaps not as close, but well within the range of the sound its jets made. He swore under his breath, looked around undecidedly, and settled on adding more fuel to the fire. He bent down for branches, and abruptly jumped up as though he had seen an adder. 'What's the matter?' Morris demanded, startled.

'That thing!' Cliteman's voice was shaky. He was staring at the wrecked midge flier on the ground before him. He darted a quick look over his shoulder, then jumped towards it, obviously intending to stamp it into the ground.

'Wait!' screamed Morris; blocking Cliteman's path.

'Out of the way!'

'No, Cliteman! You'll kill them!'

'You're damn well right I'll kill them. We're crazy to leave that thing in plain sight. Those others will come back any minute, and if they see it, wham! We're done for, man!'

'Wait!' ordered Morris in a totally different voice, a voice of command.

Cliteman stopped and stared.

Morris said tightly, 'It's murder. I won't let you do it.'

Cliteman stood poised, and his eyes were hard on the limping man. He held the twisted stick of firewood in his hand. For a moment is seemed that the stick would be a club, to strike at Morris; but there was a nearing whistle and a fleck of light that darted about their heads. Both men jumped. They had forgotten the midge jet, but the jet had not forgotten them. It came swooping in on them like an earthly plane circling living pylons; and if there had been a chance before, that chance was gone.

Perhaps it had been only curiosity that made the midge pilot come close to the quarrelling Titans; perhaps he had caught a glimpse of the wreck. Whatever, it did him in; for the stick that might have been a club became a flyswatter; Cliteman swung, as quickly, as thoughtlessly as a polar

52

relay, and slapped the prying midge plane out of the air. There was a faint ringing crunch as the tree trunk hit the plane, and a distant hiss and tiny crack as the plane slammed into the water and exploded; and that was the end of that.

'Now we are in for it,' said Cliteman after a moment. And, after a moment more, 'I'm sorry.'

Morris only shook his head. It was late to be sorry. 'Clean that fish, will you?' he said.

'Clean— What?'

'That fish,' said Morris irritably. 'Or whatever it is. We're going to have to eat it, you know. We're going to have a long night ahead of us.'

He turned his back on the other man and bent to look at the crashed midge flier that had started the trouble. They were alive after all, he saw absently; all three of the occupants were moving and one of them was chirping excitedly. Not that it mattered to Morris, not any more . . .

Picture a pair of horrid monsters, obelisk-tall, deformed beyond human experience, rampaging about Levittown or thundering in the surf at Laguna Beach. Picture them dropped from space in a queer, enormous vessel the like of which no man had ever seen, their voices a quivering diapason that hurts the ear and shakes the spine. Picture them feasting on whale sharks or such enormous offal from the sea, quarrelling among themselves, and striking out to clout an airliner in ruins from the sky.

It is no wonder, thought Morris, *that the midges don't want us around.*

But if the positions had been reversed—would we at least have tried to communicate?

But—if the positions had been reversed—would we have allowed the monsters to live at all?

Morris sighed, and blew on the chunk of greasy flesh he was holding, and forced himself to eat.

The two men ate in silence. Above them, and outward to the sea, there was a clustering swarm of midge aircraft, not approaching, but observing every move. They had begun to arrive within minutes after Cliteman had struck at the midge plane. They were waiting for something.

Whatever it was it couldn't be long in coming.

'Hurry up!' Cliteman grumbled hoarsely. Morris nodded but didn't answer; there wasn't much to say.

They had planned for a month, and the sum of their planning was this: someday they would make a break for the rocket. It would not be impossible, for between them and the spot where the rocket had crashed lay dense brush —towering jungle, by midge standards; it would be hard for the little creatures to bring much force to bear against them. On the other hand, it would not be very fruitful, for the rocket had crashed. As a plan, it had only one real advantage; it was better than nothing.

It would have been better, thought Morris with detachment, *if we could have waited until I was stronger—until the ship returned from Neighbour, and maybe another rocket might come down—until the chances were somehow better* ...

But that was exactly what was no longer possible. For there was no doubt that whatever the earthmen's status with the midges had been, the destruction of the plane had changed it for the worse.

'Morris! What the devil's that?'

Cliteman was pointing.

Something bright and fast was gliding towards them in the water. It was long—six or eight feet, easily—but not very wide. It looked rather like a mechanized small canoe, with a row of lights and brighter lights fixed forward.

Hiss, *splat*. A fat blue spark leaped from the prow of the thing towards them, fell short and sizzled in the water.

'I didn't know the midges had battleships,' said Morris in amazement, and then shook himself. 'Come on; let's get out of here!'

'Hold it!' Cliteman caught him by the shoulder, his eyes

54

huge and fearful as he stared down the beach. In the pale light from Neighbour it was hard to see what was going on. But once again there were lights, hundreds of them it seemed; they dipped and bobbed and joggled and came on. Morris saw at last what the lights belonged to. They were wheeled machines—not earthly wheels, thin in proportion to their diameter, but constructed like flabby steam rollers, creeping forward on rubbery cylinders. There were scores and hundreds of them. Tanks? Something very like tanks, at any rate; in a moment they opened fire, too, and the giants from earth were caught in a criss-cross of flying sparks. '*We're cut off!*' cried Cliteman. '*Run!*'

But it was a little late to run.

A fat blue spark caught Cliteman on the shoulder and spun him around, yelling. Morris dropped to the ground as another hissed past him, and he could smell the dry, chemical bite of ozone in his nose, taste the metallic eddy-currents in his teeth. 'They can see us in the firelight!' Cliteman yelled, and began to kick furiously at the little campfire. Burning sticks scattered into the brush, sparks flew up from the fire—redder, milder sparks than those that came from the midge weapons, but sparks that could burn all the same.

The fire from the midge tanks on the beach came in thick volleys now, and it was impossible that all of them should miss. These were no mere bee-stings like the hand weapons, Morris discovered; he yelled, holding his arm, as he discovered it. A couple of shots from these heavy weapons could easily kill.

He lifted his head. 'We've got to get out of here! Look!' The flying brands from the fire had not conveniently gone out; the brush was beginning to blaze.

'It'll give them something to think about,' Cliteman snarled, and plunged towards the mainland, bobbing and weaving and yelling. It was miraculous that he wasn't struck down by the massed fire from the beach—yet perhaps not so miraculous, for what human gunners could

55

have kept their heads in the face of a charging, bellowing monster a tenth of a mile tall? He got free, Morris following, and in a moment they were in the momentary shelter of the deep brush inland. Behind them, yellow flames and floating sparks rose up towards the bright night sky; ahead was only darkness.

Morris leaned against a twelve-foot tree, panting hoarsely. 'What—what next?' he gasped, fighting for breath.

Cliteman breathed a long, shuddering sigh. 'What do you think? We'll try for the rocket, and then—' He stopped, hesitated, swore and said roughly, 'Come on!'

Morris limped painfully after. And then? *Idiot question*, he thought wearily; there isn't any 'and then.' They might make it to the rocket and they might not; but whatever happened, there was no future for them.

He paused to catch his breath. Apart from the din Cliteman made pounding through the brush ahead, it was quiet in the woods. The blue-white light from Neighbour filtered down through the leaves. There was a sighing, whispering noise behind him that might have been the fire they left, and might have been the wind; he didn't turn his head to look. He didn't even look up at the distant overhead whistling that, beyond doubt, was the sound of midge jets looking for them. They would be hard to spot in the brush —at least until daylight.

Resolutely, he didn't think beyond daylight.

Cliteman was getting pretty far ahead. Morris stood up. He spread his fingers for a moment, and glanced at the little wrecked midge plane. It had been a foolish impulse to pick it up from the sand beside the fire. It might have been safe enough there; the little creatures would have been cooked alive. But were they any safer with him? He glanced at them; they were still moving, at least. Perhaps he should put them on the ground and leave them, he thought . . .

But he didn't. In a moment he closed his fingers over the tiny ship and limped after Cliteman.

Morris was sitting at his instrument board, transmitting the news of their arrival to Earth. He was well fed, well rested, his wounds entirely healed; the Earth signals were coming through, giving landing instructions and congratulations to the whole crew. Things were fine. The only little flaw was that, for some reason, the rocket motors of the ship were coughing explosively, jarring him, making it hard to receive the faint signal from Earth ...

'Wake up, Morris!'

He sat up with a start and looked around.

No radio instruments, no ship, no signals from Earth.

He was half propped against a tree, in the woods, and a soft rain was filtering down through the leaves overhead. Sharp coughing explosions were coming from somewhere nearby. The rockets? Then he remembered. No, not rockets. It was midge fliers, dropping their little missile-bombs, stabbing into the unseen ground beneath the tree-tops, trying to connect with Cliteman and himself. None of them were coming very close—but the midges had plenty of bombs.

Morris coughed raspingly and stood up. Cliteman was grumbling, 'It's getting light. Do you see the rocket?'

Morris bent and retrieved the little midge ship. The three occupants were still moving—more weakly, he thought.

Something was glittering, out beyond the fringes of the dense wood. Perhaps a quarter of a mile away, catching light from setting Neighbour, washed out by the beginning glow of Canopus itself.

'Is that it?'

'No, you idiot! Can't you see it's moving?' Cliteman muttered to himself, pacing back and forth, staring out. The younger man was pretty near collapse, Morris judged. That made two of them. He squinted at the glittering thing. It was moving, all right—well, that ruled out the possibility of its being the rocket. But what was it? Something low to the ground and metallic, crawling back and forth in

57

an open stretch. Large, as midge standards went—a yard or more long. Perhaps it was some sort of agricultural machinery, gang-ploughs, sowers, whatever the midges used. The small community where Morris had been a forced labourer had had nothing like it; but, of course, he hadn't seen anything like enough of the midge civilization to judge what technological heights it might attain.

He glanced up, and saw the glimmer of midge jets circling about. The distant cough of the little bombs seemed to come mostly towards the west in the direction of setting Neighbour; and looking at the patterned jets, Morris realized that most of them were over there too. Now, why should they think we're over that way? he wondered.

And then he knew.

'Cliteman! If you were a midge, where would you expect us to head for?'

Cliteman scowled fretfully. 'How the devil do I know? Oh—towards the rocket, I guess. Where else is there?'

'Nowhere else, Cliteman! So—they're probably concentrated around the rocket. And if you'll look at those jets...'

Cliteman looked surprised, then merely worried again. 'You're right, I suppose. Well—let's try that way. God knows we won't be any worse off, even if we don't find it!'

But they did.

They had to pay a price, because the midge jets were thick as wasps about a nest, but in the glimmering, pre-dawn light they saw the looming tail-rockets of their scout towering over the trees that lay between.

They paused for just a second to catch their breath, then Cliteman bellowed, 'All right, let's get going!' And he lumbered out of the shelter of the woods, Morris limping and scuttling along behind him.

It was a matter of seconds only, and then the midge aircraft had them spotted. *Thank God*, thought Morris with a part of his brain as he ran, *thank God they don't seem to have guns on the jets!* But the little buzzing craft came racing in at them as though they intended to ram, swerving off at the last moment, dropping little rice-grain objects that spun and crashed like tiny firecrackers—but louder and more dangerously than any firecrackers that Morris had ever seen.

Cliteman was roaring and flailing his arms as he ran; perhaps that helped, for the midge jets could have come closer still, and then they would not have missed. As it was they veered away short, and though the tiny bombs made ant craters fly up all about the running feet of the earthmen, and the pelting sand from the blasts stung their bare flesh, there were no direct hits. The attackers buzzed by in squads and formations and several of them made Morris duck fearfully as, Kamikazelike, they swooped in directly at his head. That would be no mere wound, the things, small as they were, had the speed and impact of a bullet. But if the pilots had intended to ram, they missed, or changed their minds; and the two men were untouched all the way across the wide sandy field with its fuzzy little growth of midge crops...

And there was the rocket.

'Hurry, hurry!' cried Cliteman over his shoulder, and Morris tried to respond:

For the midges were waiting:

Ranked about the rocket were little squares of midge troops, or police, or whatever it was in the midge race that fired electric cannon at invading earthmen. Even a dozen yards away, Morris could hear the thin cheeping as the midges caught sight of them and prepared to open fire. *Splat! Splatsplatsplatsplat!* A burst of the searing little sparks clustered about Cliteman's head and shoulders; he roared, for though most had near misses, the one that connected had brought agony with it. He stumbled and half fell against the open port of the rocket. *Splat!* Apparently it was hard for the midge gunners to bring their pieces to bear on a moving target, even so huge a one as an earthman; for the next burst stained the sides of the rocket itself. Cliteman leaped and struggled and made it inside.

Lurching after him, Morris caught confused pictures of the rocket. There had been changes! Up against the hull of the rocket there was a shiny, spiralling ramp—not to the main port, that the humans used, but to a neat, square-cut hole, burned out of the hull by the looks of it. *Of course, of course,* Morris told himself fretfully, running and dodging and panting, *of course the midges wouldn't have left it alone! Would we have left such a thing alone if it had landed in New York?* No doubt the rocket had swarmed with the little things since the first moment after they landed . . .

And what damage they might have done inside Morris didn't bother to speculate. It didn't matter; they couldn't move the rocket, couldn't escape by flying away—and lacking that it didn't matter how terrible a fight they put up, or what weapons they could contrive from the blasters and hand-guns they might find. One of them was more than a million midges in mass, but they were outnumbered not by millions but by billions . . .

And then there was no more time for thought.

The midge gunners had found the range, and he was stung by a thousand flaming sparks. Only hand weapons so far, but he had already seen that even the hand weapons could kill. They had killed Fuller, months before, and they might kill him now. He screamed and jolted forward, swerving and bobbling, and if anything saved his life it was the appearance of Cliteman at the door of the rocket, drawing part of the fire. For a moment Morris thought dazedly that Cliteman had come to his rescue, but only for a moment. He saw Cliteman's dancing, convulsing body, and knew that—of course, of course!—there had been midges even inside the rocket, waiting!

But even so—it was better inside the rocket than out. For outside it was plain death.

Morris plunged towards the door as Cliteman was plunging out. They collided and fell.

Morris jolted to the ground, and the breath left him. So this was the end, he thought wearily. Well, let it come . . .

But something was nagging at him.

He remembered what he was carrying, what he held in his hand all through the long flight, protecting it, trying to find the right place and the right time to put it down.

The wrecked midge flier!

The tiny figures inside still moved, he saw, and he was glad. With almost the last of his strength, the maddening blue sparks charring him by inches, he stretched out his hand and opened the fingers, gently—about to set the flier on the ground.

And then his fingers closed on it again.

Morris sat up, staring at the little machine. Heedless of the scorching fire from the midge weapons, heedless of the doing, singing jets overhead.

The pain no longer mattered. It was a fact of life, and there was nothing he could do about it. He put it out of his mind.

Morris set the midge flier on the ground. He stood up, raised his huge foot over it, brought it down—fast, hard, brutal . . .

And stopped. The foot, huge as Cheop's tomb above the little flier, halted and hovered, while the tiny creatures inside stared up with huge eyes.

Morris pulled back his foot. Slowly, solemnly, he shook his head—'no' to the left, 'no' to the right.

He bent, picked up the flier again, set it carefully away, and dumped to the ground.

Lord help us, he thought, *Lord help us, that's all I can do* . . .

And then he closed his eyes, and waited for the pain to end, with the end of all pain that is dying.

But death didn't come.

There was an agony and a fiery burning but not death. It was hard to tell if there were new wounds falling on Morris's ravaged back, or only the endured pain of the old ones. There was pain, all right; but bearable pain—not the cruel, killing pain that Fuller must have felt, that Morris had expected.

He opened his eyes.

The massed weapons of the midges were ranged on him; but they weren't firing.

He looked around. Overhead the midge fliers swooped and whistled; but they weren't dropping their destructive small bombs.

Morris raised himself on his arms, fearing to hope, hoping for an end to fear. Beside him, Cliteman's incredulous voice said, 'They aren't shooting at us!'

It was true. And there before them both was the answer.

The little flier that Morris had so carefully carried, so carefully set out of harm's way. There was no one in it now; but one tiny midge sat painfully on the ground beside it, looking up at them.

If the flat, huge-eyed face wore an expression, Morris couldn't read it. But what he could read beyond question was the fact that the other two were gone—to the midges manning the guns, beyond doubt. Gone to tell them that —that . . .

'Why, they must have told the others we meant no harm,' whispered Cliteman, and looked wonderingly at Morris.

Morris nodded slowly.

Cliteman pulled himself painfully to his feet. 'Morris the Destroyer,' he breathed, and there was no irony in his tone. 'Morris the Giver of Life. You showed them we didn't want to kill, and they understood.'

He helped Morris to his feet, and the two of them stood regarding the slowly advancing midges, now with their weapons turned to the ground.

'I'm glad,' said Cliteman; 'I'm glad you took such good care of the three in the plane.'

Executive Officer Yardsley, favouring his bandaged and splinted arm, squinted at his desk calculator and announced, 'We're in an orbit that'll hold us for a while, I guess. Any word from the landing party?'

'I'll check with the radio room,' said the Officer of the Deck, and dialled its combination on the intercom.

Yardsley leaned back, patting the bandages on his arm. Outside the viewscreen, bright Canopus blazed at them. It had been a rough trip, complicated with hostile inhabitants on the planet of the star called Neighbour. He was entirely ready for the long, peaceful trip back to Earth, as soon as they collected the crew of the scout rocket that had gone down to look over the Canopan planet—it couldn't be too long or too peaceful for Executive Officer Yardsley. He had made the mistake of volunteering for the landing party on the planet that circled Neighbour; and when the aborigines turned out to be large green anthropoids with Stone Age culture and surly tempers, he had been one of those who had been on the receiving end of the slung stones that greeted them.

The O.O.D. was listening with considerable interest to whatever it was the radio room had to report, Yardsley noted. At last he said, 'Good-oh, thanks,' and hung up.

'Well?' demanded Yardsley.

'Oh, they've had a ball,' the O.O.D. told him, grinning. 'The radio room just established contact, and they haven't got the whole story yet. But enough. They had a little trouble at first, but now they've established contact with the native population. Civilized, Yardsley—and they've got machines, aircraft, everything. And, oh, yes—they only average about half an inch high!'

'Half an inch high,' repeated Yardsley, remembering the green anthropoids. He sighed. 'Wouldn't you know it? I had a free choice—I could have gone with them, or I could have landed on Neighbour. Just my luck to pick the one that was *dangerous*.'

FREDERIK POHL

The Last Weapon

Edsel was in a murderous mood. He, Parke, and Faxon had spent three weeks in this part of the deadlands, breaking into every mound they came across, not finding anything, and moving on to the next. The swift Martian summer was passing, and each day became a little colder. Each day Edsel's nerves, uncertain at the best of times, had frayed a little more. Little Faxon was cheerful, dreaming of all the money they would make when they found the weapons, and Parke plodded silently along, apparently made of iron, not saying a word unless he was spoken to.

But Edsel had reached his limit. They had broken into another mound, and again there had been no sign of the lost Martian weapons. The watery sun seemed to be glaring at him, and the stars were visible in an impossibly blue sky. The afternoon cold seeped into Edsel's insulated suit, stiffening his joints, knotting his big muscles.

Quite suddenly, Edsel decided to kill Parke. He had disliked the silent man since they had formed the partnership on Earth. He disliked him even more than he despised Faxon.

Edsel stopped.

'Do you know where we're going?' he asked Parke, his voice ominously low.

Parke shrugged his slender shoulders negligently. His pale, hollow face showed no trace of expression.

'Do you?' Edsel asked.

Parke shrugged again.

A bullet in the head, Edsel decided, reaching for his gun.

'Wait!' Faxon pleaded, coming up between them. 'Don't fly off, Edsel. Just think of all the money we can make when we find the weapons!' The little man's eyes glowed

65

at the thought. 'They're right around here somewhere, Edsel. The next mound, maybe.'

Edsel hesitated, glaring at Parke. Right now he wanted to kill more than anything else in the world. If he had known it would be like this, when they formed the company on Earth ... It had seemed so easy then. He had the plaque, the one which told where a cache of the fabulous lost Martian weapons were. Parke was able to read the Martian script, and Faxon could finance the expedition. So, he had figured all they'd have to do would be to land on Mars and walk up to the mound where the stuff was hidden.

Edsel had never been off Earth before. He hadn't counted on the weeks of freezing, starving on concentrated rations, always dizzy from breathing thin, tired air circulating through a replenisher. He hadn't thought about the sore, aching muscles you get, dragging your way through the thick Martian brush.

All he had thought about was the price a government— any government—would pay for those legendary weapons.

'I'm sorry,' Edsel said, making up his mind suddenly. 'This place gets me. Sorry I blew up, Parke. Lead on.'

Parke nodded, and started again. Faxon breathed a sigh of relief, and followed Parke.

After all, Edsel thought. I can kill them anytime.

They found the correct mound in mid-afternoon, just as Edsel's patience was wearing thin again. It was a strange, massive affair, just as the script had said. Under a few inches of dirt was metal. The men scraped and found a door.

'Here, I'll blast it open,' Edsel said, drawing his revolver.

Parke pushed him aside, turned the handle and opened the door.

Inside was a tremendous room. And there, row upon gleaming row, were the legendary lost weapons of Mars, the missing artifacts of Martian civilisation.

The three men stood for a moment, just looking. Here was the treasure that men had almost given up looking for. Since man had landed on Mars, the ruins of great cities had been explored. Scattered across the plains were ruined vehicles, art forms, tools everything indicating the ghost of a titanic civilisation, a thousand years beyond Earth's. Patiently deciphered scripts had told of the great wars ravaging the surface of Mars. The scripts stopped too soon, though, because nothing told what happened to the Martians. There hadn't been an intelligent being on Mars for several thousand years. Somehow, all animal life on the planet had been obliterated.

And, apparently, the Martians had taken their weapons with them.

These lost weapons, Edsel knew, were worth their weight in radium. There just wasn't anything like them.

The men went inside. Edsel picked up the first thing his hand reached. It looked like a .45, but bigger. He went to the door and pointed the weapon at a shrub on the plain.

'Don't fire it,' Faxon said, as Edsel took aim. 'It might backfire or something. Let the government men fire them, after we sell.'

Edsel squeezed the trigger. The shrub, 75 feet away, erupted in a bright red flash.

'Not bad,' Edsel said, patting the gun. He put it down and reached for another.

'Please, Edsel,' Faxon said, squinting nervously at him. 'There's no need to try them out. You might set off an atomic bomb or something.'

'Shut up,' Edsel said, examining the weapon for a firing stud.

'Don't shoot any more,' Faxon pleaded. He looked to Parke for support, but the silent man was watching Edsel.

'You know, something in this place might have been responsible for the destruction of the Martian race. You wouldn't want to set it off again, would you?'

Edsel watched a spot on the plain glow with heat as he fired at it.

'Good stuff.' He picked up another, rod-shaped instrument. The cold was forgotten. Edsel was perfectly happy now, playing with all the shiny things.

'Let's get started,' Faxon said, moving towards the door.

'Started? Where?' Edsel demanded. He picked up another glittering weapon, curved to fit his wrist and hand.

'Back to the port,' Faxon said. 'Back to sell this stuff, like we planned. I figure we can ask just about any price, any price at all. A government would give billions for weapons like these.'

'I've changed my mind,' Edsel said. Out of the corner of his eye he was watching Parke. The slender man was walking between the stacks of weapons, but so far he hadn't touched any.

'Now listen,' Faxon said, glaring at Edsel. 'I financed this expedition. We planned on selling the stuff. I have a right to—well, perhaps not.'

The untried weapon was pointed squarely at his stomach.

'What are you going to do?' he asked, trying not to look at the gun.

'To hell with selling it,' Edsel said, leaning against the cave wall where he could also watch Parke. 'I figure I can use this stuff myself.' He grinned broadly, still watching both men.

'I can outfit some of the boys back home. With the stuff that's here, we can knock over one of those little governments in Central America easy. I figure we could hold it forever.'

'Well', Faxon said, watching the gun, 'I don't want to be a party to that sort of thing. Just count me out.'

'All right,' Edsel said.

'Don't worry about me talking,' Faxon said quickly. 'I won't. I just don't want to be in on any shooting or killing. So I think I'll go back.'

'Sure,' Edsel said. Parke was standing to one side, examining his fingernails.

'If you get that kingdom set up, I'll come down,' Faxon said, grinning weakly. 'Maybe you can make me a duke or something.'

'I think I can arrange that.'

'Swell. Good luck.' Faxon waved his hand and started to walk away. Edsel let him get 20 feet, then aimed the new weapon and pressed the stud.

The gun didn't make any noise; there was no flash, but Faxon's arm was neatly severed. Quickly, Edsel pressed the stud again and swung the gun down on Faxon. The little man was chopped in half, and the ground on either side of him was slashed, also.

Edsel turned, realising that he had left his back exposed to Parke. All the man had to do was pick up the nearest gun and blaze away. But Parke was just standing there, his arms folded over his chest.

'That beam will probably cut through anything,' Parke said. 'Very useful.'

Edsel had a wonderful half hour, running back and forth to the door with different weapons. Parke made no move to touch anything, but watched with interest. The ancient Martian arms were as good as new, apparently unaffected by their thousands of years of disuse. There were many blasting weapons, of various designs and capabilities. Then heat and radiation guns, marvellously compact things. There were weapons which would freeze and weapons which would burn; others which would crumble, cut, coagulate, paralyse, and do any of the other things to snuff out life.

'Let's try this one,' Parke said. Edsel, who had been on the verge of testing an interesting-looking three-barrelled rifle, stopped.

'I'm busy,' he said.

'Stop playing with those toys. Let's have a look at some real stuff.'

Parke was standing near a squat black machine on wheels. Together they tugged it outside. Parke watched while Edsel moved the controls. A faint hum started deep in the machine. Then a blue haze formed around it. The haze spread as Edsel manipulated the controls until it surrounded the two men.

'Try a blaster on it,' Parke said. Edsel picked up one of the explosive pistols and fired. The charge was absorbed by the haze. Quickly he tested three others. They couldn't pierce the blue glow.

'I believe,' Parke said softly, 'this will stop an atomic bomb. This is a force field.'

Edsel turned it off and they went back inside. It was growing dark in the cave as the sun neared the horizon.

'You know,' Edsel said, 'you're a pretty good guy, Parke. You're OK.'

'Thanks,' Parke said, looking over the mass of weapons.

'You don't mind my cutting down Faxon, do you? He was going straight to the government.'

'On the contrary, I approve.'

'Swell. I figure you must be OK. You could have killed me when I was killing Faxon.' Edsel didn't add that it was what he would have done.

Parke shrugged his shoulders.

'How would you like to work on this kingdom deal with me?' Edsel asked, grinning. 'I think we could swing it. Get ourselves a nice place, plenty of girls, lots of laughs. What do you think?'

'Sure,' Parke said. 'Count me in.' Edsel slapped him on the shoulder, and they went through the ranks of weapons.

'All these are pretty obvious,' Parke said as they reached the end of the room. 'Variations on the others.'

At the end of the room was a door. There were letters in Martian script engraved on it.

'What's that stuff say?' Edsel asked.

'Something about "final weapons",' Parke told him, squinting at the delicate tracery. 'A warning to stay out,' He opened the door. Both men started to step inside, then recoiled suddenly.

Inside was a chamber fully three times the size of the room they had just left. And filling the great room, as far as they could see, were soldiers. Gorgeously dressed, fully armed, the soldiers were motionless, statuelike.

They were not alive.

There was a table by the door, and on it were three things. First, there was a sphere about the size of a man's fist, with a calibrated dial set in it. Beside that was a shining helmet. And next was a small, black box with Martian script on it.

'Is it a burial place?' Edsel whispered, looking with awe at the strong unearthly faces of the Martian soldiery. Parke, behind him, didn't answer.

Edsel walked to the table and picked up the sphere. Carefully he turned the dial a single notch.

'What do you think it's supposed to do?' he asked Parke. 'Do you think—' Both men gasped, and moved back.

The lines of fighting men had moved. Men in ranks swayed, then came to attention. But they no longer held the rigid posture of death. The ancient fighting men were alive.

One of them, in an amazing uniform of purple and silver, came forward and bowed to Edsel.

'Sir, your troops are ready.' Edsel was too amazed to speak.

'How can you live after thousands of years?' Parke answered. 'Are you Martians?'

'We are the servants of the Martians,' the soldier said. Parke noticed that the soldier's lips hadn't moved. The man was telepathic. 'Sir, we are Synthetics.'

'Whom do you obey?' Parke asked.

'The Activator, sir. Our only desire is to serve you and to fight.' The soldiers in the ranks nodded approvingly.

'Lead us into battle, sir!'

'I sure will!' Edsel said, finally regaining his senses. 'I'll show you boys some fighting, you can bank on that!'

The soldiers cheered him, solemnly, three times. Edsel grinned, looking at Parke.

'What do the rest of these numbers do?' Edsel asked. But the soldier was silent. The question was evidently beyond his built-in knowledge.

'It might activate other Synthetics,' Parke said. 'There are probably more chambers underground.'

'Brother!' Edsel shouted. '*Will* I lead you into battle!' Again the soldiers cheered, three solemn cheers.

'Put them to sleep and let's make some plans,' Parke said. Dazed, Edsel turned the switch back. The soldiers froze again into immobility.

'Come on outside.'

'Right.'

'And bring that stuff with you.' Edsel picked up the shining helmet and the black box and followed Parke outside. The sun had almost disappeared now, and there were black shadows over the red land. It was bitterly cold, but neither man noticed.

'Did you hear what they said, Parke? Did you hear it? They said I was their leader! With men like those—' He laughed at the sky. With those soldiers, those weapons, nothing could stop him. He'd really stock his land— prettiest girls in the world, and would he have a time!'

'I'm a general!' Edsel shouted, and slipped the helmet over his head. How do I look, Parke? Don't I look like a —' He stopped. He was hearing a voice in his ears, whispering, muttering. What was it saying?

'. . . *damned idiot, with his little dream of a kingdom. Power like this is for a man of genius, a man who can re-make history. Myself!'*

'Who's talking? That's you isn't it, Parke?' Edsel realised suddenly that the helmet allowed him to listen in on thoughts. He didn't have time to consider what a weapon this would be for a ruler.

Parke shot him neatly through the back with a gun he had been holding all the time.

'What an idiot,' Parke told himself, slipping the helmet on his head. A kingdom! All the power in the world, and he dreamed of a little kingdom!' He glanced back at the cave.

'With those troops—the force field—and the weapons— I can take over the world.' He said it coldly, knowing it was a fact. He turned to go back to the cave to activate the Synthetics, but stopped first to pick up the little black box Edsel had carried.

Engraved on it, in flowing Martian script, was 'The Last Weapon'.

I wonder what it could be, Parke asked himself. He had let Edsel live long enough to try out all the others; no use chancing a misfire himself. It was too bad he hadn't lived long enough to try out this one, too.

Of course, I really don't need it, he told himself. He had plenty. But this might make the job a lot easier, a lot safer. Whatever it was, it was bound to be good.

Well, he told himself, let's see what the Martians considered their last weapon. He opened the box.

A vapour drifted out, and Parke threw the box from him, thinking about poison gas.

The vapour mounted, drifted haphazardly for a while, then began to coalesce. It spread, grew and took shape.

In a few seconds, it was complete, hovering over the box. It glimmered white in the dying light, and Parke saw that it was just a tremendous mouth, topped by a pair of unblinking eyes.

'Ho ho,' the mouth said. 'Protoplasm!' * It drifted to the body of Edsel. Parke lifted a blaster and took careful aim.

'Quiet protoplasm,' the thing said, nuzzling Edsel's body.

* Living matter.

73

'I like quiet protoplasm.' It took down the body in a single gulp.

Parke fired, blasting a ten-foot hole in the ground. The giant mouth drifted out of it, chuckling.

'It's been so long,' it said.

Parke was clenching his nerves in a forged grip. He refused to let himself become panicked. Calmly he activated the force field, forming a blue sphere around himself.

Still chuckling, the thing drifted through the blue haze.

Parke picked up the weapon Edsel had used on Faxon, feeling the well-balanced piece swing up in his hand. He backed to one side of the force field as the thing approached, and turned on the beam.

The thing kept coming.

'Die, die!' Parke screamed, his nerves breaking.

But the thing came on, grinning broadly.

'I like *quiet* protoplasm,' the thing said as its gigantic mouth converged on Parke.

'But I also like *lively* protoplasm.'

It gulped once, then drifted out of the other side of the field, looking anxiously around for the millions of units of protoplasm, as there had been in the old days.

ROBERT SHECKLEY

The Attic Express

In the evenings they climbed the steep narrow stairway to the big room under the roof. Hector Coley went up eagerly and alertly. The boy followed his father draggingly. In the family it had always been called 'Brian's room', but to Brian it seemed that his father's presence filled it.

It was a long room, with low sidewalls and a ceiling like the lower half of an A. There was a large water-tank at one end: the rest of the space was 'Brian's'.

Coley ran the trains. The boy looked on.

Sometimes, when his father was absorbed, attending to midget couplings, rearranging a length of track, wiring up a tiny house so that it could be lit from inside, he looked away, and merely watched the single square of attic window gently darken.

Coley hated Brian to lose interest. He would say irritably: 'I can't understand you, Brian, beggared if I can! You know something? Some boys would give an arm to have the run of a playroom like this one I've built for you.'

The boy would shift his gaze and rub his hands together nervously. He would stoop forward hastily and peer at all parts of the track. 'Make it go through the crossing,' he would say, to appease his father. But even before the magnificent little Fleischmann engine challenged the gradient to the crossing—which would involve the delicious manoeuvre of braking two or three small cars—his eye would be away again, after a moth on the wall, or a cloud veiling the moon.

'It defeats me,' Coley would say later to his wife, 'he shows no interest in anything. Sometimes I don't get a word out of him all evening unless I drag it out of him.'

'Perhaps he's not old enough yet,' she would reply diffidently, 'you know I think I'd find it a little difficult to manage myself—all those signals and control switches and lights going on and off and trains going this way and that. I'm glad I'm never asked to work out anything more complicated than a Fair Isle knitting pattern.'

'You miss the point,' said Coley impatiently, 'I'm not expecting him to synchronize the running times of ten trains, and keep them all safely on the move, but I would like a spark of enthusiasm to show now and again. I mean, I give up hours of my time, not to speak of money running into thousands, to give him a lay-out which I'm willing to wager a couple of bob can't be matched in any home in Britain, and he can't even do me the courtesy of listening to me when I explain something. It's not good enough.'

'I know, dear, how you feel, but at ten I do feel it's a little . . .'

'Oh, rubbish,' exclaimed Coley, 'ten's a helluvan age. At ten I could dismantle a good watch and put it together again better than new.'

'You are exceptional, dear. Not everyone has your mechanical bent. I expect Brian's will show itself in time.'

'There again, will it? His reports all read the same: "Could do much better if he applied himself more . . . doesn't get his teeth into it . . ." and so on till I could give him a jolly good hiding. No, Meg, say what you like, it's plain to me that the boy simply won't try.'

'In some subjects he's probably a little better than in others.'

'Nonsense,' said Coley energetically, 'anybody can do anything, if they want to enough.'

One evening, after listening to his complaints meekly for a while, she suddenly interrupted him:

'Where is he now?'

'Where I left him. I've given him the new express in its box. I want to see whether he's got enough gumption to set it out on the track with the right load. If I find it's still in the box when I get back . . .'

'Yes, dear,' she said, surprising him with her vehemence, 'why don't you bring the matter to a head? It's getting on my nerves a bit, you know, sitting down here reading and watching television, and imagining you struggling. If he's not really interested, then could we have an end to all this? I know the railways are your pride, but honestly I'd rather see them scrapped than listen to any more of this.'

He was astonished. He went back upstairs without a word.

The boy was squatting, with his face cupped in one hand, elbow on knee. His straight brown hair fell forward and half obscured his face. The other arm dangled loosely, and the forefinger of his hand moved an empty light truck to and fro a few inches on the floor.

The express was on the rails. Brian had it at the head of an extraordinarily miscellaneous collection of waggons: Pullmans, goods trucks, restaurant cars, breakdown waggons, timber trucks, oil canisters—anything, obviously, which had come to hand.

'Sit down at the control panel, Brian,' snapped Coley.

The boy did not reply, but he did what he was told.

'I want you to run this express tonight,' said Coley, 'and I'm not going to lift a finger to help. But I'll be fair, too, I won't criticize. I'll stay right out of it. In fact for all you know I might as well be on the train itself. Think of me being on it, that's it, and run it accordingly . . .'

He was trying to keep the anger and disappointment out of his voice. The boy half turned a moment, and looked at him steadily, then he resumed his scrutiny of the control panel.

'. . . take your time . . . think it all out . . . don't do anything hastily . . . keep your wits about you . . . remember all I've taught you . . . that's a gorgeous little model I've got there for you . . . I'm on board . . . up on the footplate if you like . . . we'll have a gala and just have it lit with the illuminations of the set itself . . . give me time to get aboard . . . I'm in your hands, son. . . .'

Coley stood on the railway line. The giant express faced him, quiet, just off the main line. He started to walk along the track towards it.

He felt no astonishment at finding himself in scale with the models. *Anyone can do anything, if they want to enough.* He'd wished to drive a model, from the footplate, and here he was walking towards it.

But at the first step he took, he sank almost up to his knees in the ballast below the track. It was, after all, only foam rubber. He grinned. 'I'll have to remember things like that,' he told himself.

He stopped by the engine and looked up at the boiler. He whistled softly between his teeth, excited by so much beauty. What a lovely job these Germans made of anything they tackled. Not a plate out of line. A really sumptuous, genuine, top of the form job! He wished the maker a ton of good dinners. The thing was real, not a doubt.

He stepped on through tiny, incisive pebbles of sand, treading cautiously. One or two had threatened to cut into his shoes. Looking down, he noticed a right-angled bar of metal, gleaming at his feet. He realised in a moment that it must be one of the staples which had held the engine's box together. Chuckling over his own drollness at playing the game to the full, he picked up the bar and with an effort almost succeeded in straightening it right out. Then he advanced on the wheel and tapped it. The wheel was, of course, sound. He ran his hand over the virgin wheel. He lifted his arm and placed his hand against the smooth gloss of the boiler. He could do that because it was quite cold. He smiled again: that took away a bit of the realism, to think of a steam engine run on electricity. When you were down to scale, it seemed you noticed these things.

Then he frowned as he noticed something else. The coupling of the first carriage, a Pullman, could not have been properly made up by Brian. The first wheels were well clear of the rails. He ran past the tender to have a look. Sure enough. Damn careless of him! He was about to call out to Brian, when he remembered his promise to say nothing, and thought he'd make the correction himself. It was just a matter of sliding the arm across until the spoke fell into the slot in the rear of the tender. The remainder of the fastening was simple. He jabbed the lever in under the arm and strained to shift the carriage.

After a minute, during which the carriage swayed a bit but did not move, he stopped and took off his coat. He was still in his office suit. He wished he were in his old flannels and lumberjack shirt, but at least he hadn't changed into slippers. Sweat trickled down his back. He hadn't had much time for exercise lately, though his usual practice was conditioning on the links, alternate fifteen yards running and walking, for eighteen holes. Without clubs, of course.

He hurled himself at it again, bracing his full weight against the lever. Suddenly the arm shifted, and skidded over the new surface on which it rested. The spoke found the slot, and the whole carriage crashed into position on the rails. The lever flicked off with rending force, and one spinning end struck him under the arm, just near the shoulder.

He thought he would be sick with the pain. All feeling went out of his arm, except at the point of impact. There was plenty of feeling, all vividly unpleasant. Almost mechanically he leant down and picked up his jacket. Trailing it, he tottered back to the engine, and slowly hoisted himself into the cab. There he leant over one of the immobile levers until he had partially recovered.

He was still palpating his startled flesh, and establishing that no bone was broken, when, without any preliminary warnings, the train suddenly jerked into motion. Wheeling round, he managed to save himself from falling by hooking himself into the window of the cab. He looked for his son, to signal that he was not quite ready yet. Even without the blow he had just sustained he would have liked a few more minutes to adjust himself to the idea of being part of a model world, before the journey began.

But he couldn't at first see where he was. In this fantastic landscape, lit but not warmed by three suns, all the familiar features had undergone a change. The sensation resembled in some way that which comes to a man who visits a district he knows well by daylight, for the first time after dark.

In the direct light of those three suns, an overhead monster and two wall brackets, everything glittered. Plain to Coley, but less noticeable to the boy at the table on which was spread the control panel, were separate shadows of differing intensity radiating from every upright object. But the objects themselves sparkled. Light came flashing and twinkling and glancing from the walls and roofs of the houses, from the foliage of the trees, from the heaps of coal by the sidings, from the clothes and faces of the men and women. The lines of the railway themselves shone, twisting and turning a hundred times amongst windmills and farms and garages and fields and stations, all throwing back this aggressive, stupefying brilliance of light. Coley screwed up his eyes and tried to work it out. The train slipped forward smoothly, gaining momentum. The boy hadn't made a bad job of the start, anyway. Perhaps he took in more than I imagined, said Coley to himself.

He fixed his eye on a vast grey expanse, stretching away parallel to the course they were on, and appearing like a long rectangular field of some kind of close undergrowth with curling tops. What the devil could that be? He didn't remember putting down anything like that. Whatever it was, it didn't look anything like the real thing, now that he was down to scale. A breeze stirred small clumps which seemed to ride clear of the rest, and it came to him that, of course, this was the strip of carpet he'd laid down on one side of the room, always insisting that people should walk only on this if possible, to prevent breakages.

If that was the carpet . . . he rushed across to the other window, just in time before the engine started to take a
80

corner, to see the top of his son's head bent over the controls.

It was miles away! So huge! So . . . dare he admit it to himself . . . grotesque! The line of his parting, running white across his scalp, showed to the man in the cab like a streak in a forest, a blaze consequent upon roadmaking. A house could have been hidden behind the hair falling across his forehead. The shadow of his son on the burning white sky behind was like a storm cloud.

Brian disappeared from his view as the track curled, and Coley shook his head, as if he could clear away these images as a dog rattles away drops of water from its fur. 'It's not like me to imagine things,' said Coley fiercely. All the same, drops of moisture stood out on the back of the hand which clutched a lever.

He sensed a slight acceleration. The telegraph poles were coming by now at more than one a second. He felt the use of his injured arm returning, and with it a return of self-confidence. 'I wonder if, when I return to my normal size, the bruise will be to scale or be only, quite literally, a scratch?'

He was about to resume his jacket, since the wind was now considerable, when the train turned again and he lost his balance. In falling, the jacket fell from his hand, and was whipped away out of the cab.

Unhurt by his fall, but irritated by the loss of the jacket, Coley pulled himself to his feet and swore: 'Hell of a lot of bends on this railway,' as if he were perceiving it for the first time, 'anyway, that doesn't matter so much, I can put up with a fresh wind for a while if he'd only think what all this bloody light is doing to my eyes. Tone down the ruddy glare, can't you?'

As if in answer, the suns were extinguished.

For an instant the succeeding blackness was complete.

The express forged almost noiselessly through the dark. Coley fumbled for handholds. 'That's a bit inefficient,' he muttered. But the totality of darkness was not for long.

Simultaneously, and Coley imagined Brian studying the switches, all the lights in the houses and stations and farms and windmills, and so forth, were flipped on.

'That's really rather nice to look at!' said Coley, appreciatively. 'I always knew I'd done a good job there, but it's only now that I can see just how good. I don't think they can complain there,' he went on. 'I think they'd admit I've looked after that little creature comfort.' He was referring to the little people with whom he had populated the world in which the attic express was running.

He also thought, as the walls of the attic vanished altogether: 'If he hasn't noticed that the old man's no longer sitting in the armchair behind him, he's not likely to now. It would be rather good to slip back into the chair before the lights go up again. I'll have to watch my moment as soon as he's had enough and stops the express.'

They sped through a crossing. Coley, looking down on it, and at the figures massed by the gate, observed a solitary figure in a patch of light, waving. Whimsically, he waved back. The expression on the face of the waving man was one of jubilation. His smile reached, literally, from ear to ear. 'A cheery chappie,' remarked Coley. He was beginning to enjoy himself.

At a comfortable pace the express swung into the long straight which led into the area described on the posters and signboards as Coleyville. It was the largest and best equipped of the five stations. Coley thought that Brian must see it as an inevitable stop. Interesting to see whether he could bring it in to a nice easy check. The passengers might be assumed to be taking down their suitcases, and dragging on their coats, and would be resentful at being overbalanced.

Far up ahead Coley could see the platform approaching. He could make out the long line of people waiting to climb aboard. A representative body of folk, thought Coley, I got in a good cross-section of the travelling public for Coleyville. Then, flashing down the hill, on the road

82

which would cross the track just this side of the station in a scissors intersection, Coley saw an open sports car. It was coming down at a frightening speed, and should reach the junction just as the express went through.

'The young monkey!' breathed Coley, 'he must be getting into the swing of it.' For a moment he tensed, until he remembered that on this crossing there was a synchronization which would automatically brake the car. A high, whining metallic noise filled his ears from the single rail of the roadster, which abruptly cut off as the car was stopped.

'From eighty to rest in a split second,' thought Coley, 'that's not too realistic. Not the boy's fault, but I'll have to see if I can't improve on that.' He also noticed, as the express moved slowly through the crossing, that there were no features on the face of the roadster's driver. Not even eyes! 'No use telling you to look where you're going!' shouted Coley. The square-shouldered driver sat upright and motionless, waiting for the express to be out of his way.

The express stopped at Coleyville.

'Perfect!' exclaimed Coley, 'just perfect!' He wished he could shake Brian's hand. The boy must care after all, to be able to handle the stuff in this way. His heart swelled. He thought for a moment of stepping off at Coleyville and watching from the outside for a while, and then pick her up again next time she stopped. But he couldn't be sure the boy would bring her round again on the same line. And this was far too exhilarating an adventure to duck out of now. He stayed.

He leant out of the cab and looked down the platform at the people waiting. It was a mild surprise to him that no one moved. There they stood, their baggage in their hands or at their feet, waiting for trains, and doing nothing about it when one came. He saw the guard, staring at him. The guard's face was a violent maroon colour, and the front part of one foot was missing. He had doubtless good reasons for drinking heavily. Immediately behind him was a lovely blonde, about seven feet high, and with one breast considerably larger than the other, but otherwise delicious to look at. At her side was a small boy in suit and school cap. He had the face of a middle-aged man. Farther on down a toothless mastiff gambolled, at the end of a leash held by a gentleman in city suit and homburg. He was flawless, but for the fact that he had omitted to put on collar and tie.

Coley rubbed the side of his nose with his index finger. 'I never expected to discover that you had such curious characters,' he said ruefully. The guard stared at him balefully, the blonde proudly. The express moved out of the station. Coley took his shoe off and hammered the glass out of the right-hand foreport. It was too opaque for proper vision. He smiled as he thought of the faces of the makers if he should write to them criticizing. Being Germans, they'd take it seriously, and put the matter right in future.

Beyond Coleyville the track wound through low hills. Coleyville was a dormitory town, but on the outskirts were some prosperous farms whose flocks could be seen all about the hills. A well–appointed country club lay at the foot of the high land which bordered the east wall, which was continued in illusion by a massive photograph of the Pennines which Coley had had blown up to extend most of the length of the wall. It was, in Coley's view, one of the most agreeable and meticulously arranged districts in his entire lay-out.

By the fences of the farms stood children, waving. Yokels waved. Lambs and dogs frisked. A water-mill turned slowly. It ran on a battery, but looked very real. Plump milkmaids meandered to and fro. 'Lovely spot for a holiday,' thought urban Coley, sentimentally. He leant far out of the cab window to have a better view of the whole wide perspective, and almost had his head taken off by a passing goods train.

It came up very softly, passing on the outside of a curve.

Coley withdrew his head only because he happened to catch a slight shadow approach.

He leant his face against the cold metal by his window. 'Idiot!' he said to himself in fright and anger.

The goods train went by at a smart clip. There were only about five trucks on it, all empty.

'Steady, old chap!' he apostrophized his son, under his breath, 'don't take on too much all at once.'

For the first time it occurred to him that it might be a good thing to be ready to skip clear in the event of danger. Brian was operating very sensibly at present, but a lapse in concentration. . . . A vague chill passed down Coley's spine.

He looked back at the train on which he was travelling. It might be better to pick his way to the rear coaches.

He took three strides and launched himself on to the tender. Landing, he tore his trousers on the rough surface which represented coal nuts. It was very slippery and he almost slid right over it altogether, but he contrived to dig toes and hands into the depressions and check himself.

The express was moving along an embankment. Below him he could see the figures of young women in bathing suits disporting themselves about a glass swimming pool. Uniformed waiters stood obsequiously about, handing drinks to shirt-sleeved gentlemen under beach umbrellas. In the context of night-time the scene appeared macabre and hinting of recondite pleasures, particularly when the white legs of one of the beauties, protruding from under a glistering, russet bush, were taken into account. She could have been a corpse, and none of the high-lifers caring.

Coley wriggled forward cautiously over the hard black lumps. He wished now he'd stayed where he was, since the strong wind was more than he had allowed for.

He scrambled to a sitting position on the hard, pointed surface of the tender. Beyond the country club, looking ahead, were the mountains. He sought about for the secure footholds he'd need before making his leap off the tender into the gaping doorway of the Pullman behind, but decided to postpone the effort until the express had passed through the long tunnel. There was a long gentle declivity on the far side, a gradient of $1/248$ he'd posted it, and he'd have a more stable vehicle to jump to. Besides, in the tunnel it would be dark.

He remembered himself one Sunday morning, making the mountain secure above the tunnel. The trouble he'd had with that material, nailing it in firmly without damaging any of the features of the landscape built on to it.

Those nails!

Some must protrude into the tunnel itself! He'd never troubled himself about them. There had always been plenty of clearance for the trains themselves. But, for him, perched on top of the tender? He looked round desperately to see if he might still have time to make his leap.

But he had remembered too late. The tunnel sucked them in like a mouth. He rolled flat on his face and prayed.

It was not completely dark, though very nearly so. A vague glow came through at one section where a tricky bit of building had been finally effected with painted canvas, and in it he was lucky to spot one of the nails and wriggle clear. The other he never saw. The point, aimed perpendicularly downwards, just caught his collar, as it arched upward over his straining neck.

He was jerked up bodily. It was very swift. He had no time to do anything about it. For a second he seemed to be suspended on the very tip of the nail, then the shirt tore and he was delivered back on the train.

He landed with a vicious thump on some part of a waggon some distance below roof-level. Something drove like the tip of a boot into his knee and he doubled over against what might be a rail. He clung to it. He couldn't tell where he was, but he could hear a wheel clicking furiously beneath him. Gasping from the pain of his knee, and a dull throb between the shoulder blades, he hung on and waited for the end of the tunnel and light.

It came suddenly.

His first feeling was relief that he had been thrown almost on the very spot he had chosen to jump to before the train entered the tunnel. But this was succeeded by a stab of anguish from his back as he raised himself to his feet in the doorway of the Pullman. He put his hand behind his back and found first that his shirt had split all the way to his trousers. He allowed it to flow down his arms, and held it in one hand while he probed his back with the other.

'Ye Gods,' he murmured shakily as he examined his hand after feeling his wound, 'I must be bleeding like a stuck pig!'

Slowly he converted his shirt into a great bandage, wrapping it around his chest, under his armpits and tying it below his chin, like a bra in reverse. While he was doing this, grunting as much from astonishment at his predicament as from pain, the express accelerated, and as it thundered along the decline his horror at this was added to the confusion of his feelings.

'I must stop this,' he said thickly, 'I must signal the boy to cut the power off.' He reeled into the Pullman. On the far side he seemed to remember there was a flat truck with nothing on it but a couple of logs. Perhaps if he got astride one of them, he could make himself be seen.

From nowhere appeared the colossal torso of a man. It was white coated, but the face was mottled, a sort of pie-bald, with only one deeply sunken eye, and the other the faintest smear at the point of the normal cheekbone.

'Get away! Get away!' screamed Coley, striking out at it wildly. One of his blows landed high on the man's chest. He teetered a moment, and then, without bending, went over on his back. The material from which he was made was very light. He was no more than amalgam of plastics and painted hat.

Coley looked down at the prostrate dummy and rubbed his bloodied hand over his forehead. 'No sense in getting hysterical,' he warned himself. He stepped over the prostrate figure, twisting to avoid the outstretched arm. He observed with revulsion that the fingers on the hand were webbed, a glittering duck-egg blue. Coley ran his tongue over his lips, tasting blood. 'Take a brace,' he admonished himself, reverting to the slang of his schooldays, 'don't let your imagination run away with you.'

He staggered amongst the conclaves of seated gentlemen, for ever impassive and at their ease in armchairs, content with the society in which they found themselves, unimpressed by the increasing momentum of the express, welded to their very chairs. Coley shot a glance over the gleaming carapace of one stern hock-drinker and out through the window. The variety of the landscape was flickering by with alarming speed, becoming a gale of altering colours. The coach was beginning to sway.

Coley broke into a run. The roar below him apprised him that the express was travelling over the suspension bridge. The bridge had been his pride, a labour of months, not bought whole, but built from wire and plywood in his leisure hours. He had no time now for gloating.

'I must get him to see me, or I'm done for.'

But beyond the Pullman, he found another waggon, a restaurant car. In his haste he had forgotten that one. He dashed down the aisle, grabbing tables to steady himself against the rocking of the train as he went. They must be up to seventy now, or rather about four miles an hour, he realised with bitterness.

Leaning a moment over one of the tables, he saw that the lamps in the centre were bulky, heavy-looking objects. He heaved tentatively at one of them, and it snapped off at the base. The diners, with their hands in their laps, stared on across the table at each other, untroubled by the onslaught of this wild-eyed Englishman. The Englishman, naked to the waist, his shirt sleeves dangling red and filthy down his chest, his body flaming now with a dozen bruises, stood over them a second clutching the lamp to him, panting heavily, then turned away and reeled on down the aisle. Down his retreating back the blood was flowing now freely. The shirt was inadequate to check it as it escaped from the savage wound he had sustained in the tunnel.

This time when he emerged at the doorway of the carriage he found himself looking at the open truck on which were chained four logs. He flung the lampstand ahead of him and it landed satisfyingly between two of the logs. He gathered his ebbing strength for the jump.

He was just able to make it. He caught his foot in one of the chains in mid-flight and crashed down on his face, but he saved himself from disaster by flinging one arm round a log. He sat up immediately and looked about him.

For a moment his vision was partly blocked as yet another train flashed by in the opposite direction. 'Oh, God, what's he playing at?' whispered Coley, 'he can't handle so many trains at once!'

The express was almost at the end of the long straight. It slowed for the curve right, at the bottom. For a brief time after that it would be running directly under the control panel at which Brian was sitting. That would be his chance to make an impression. He hauled himself astride the top log and waited.

The express took the curve at a reduced pace, but squealing slightly nevertheless. Coley could sense most of the load concentrate on the inner wheels. Then he could see his son above him.

He waved frantically.

Brian seemed to rise slightly from his chair. His shadow leapt gigantically ahead of him, stretching forward and up on the slanting ceiling. Behind his head the glare of the Anglepoise lamp was almost unbearable. Coley was unable to make out the features of his son at all: there was only the silhouette. He couldn't tell if he had noticed anything.

With almost despairing violence he flung the lamp. He saw it speed in a low parabola out over the road which ran parallel to the track, bounce on the white space of Brian's shin exposed above his sock, and vanish in the darkness

89

beyond. The enormous figure rose farther, towering now above the speeding express. Coley was sure now that he had been seen. He made desperate motions with his hands, indicating that he would like a total shut-down of power. The boy waved. Coley turned sick. He stared down at his hands, pathetic little signals of distress. The probability was that the boy couldn't even see them.

But he should have been aware that something was wrong. Surely he must see that.

They tore through another station. They were taking the curves now at speed. They flashed across the scores of intersecting rails of the marshalling yard. The noise was like machine-gun fire. He saw another unit come into play: a two-car diesel slipped away south in a coquettish twinkle of chromium.

'He's showing off,' thought Coley grimly, 'he's going to try to bring every bloody train we've got into motion.'

He knew now that the only way he could save himself would be somehow to get off the train. If only he didn't feel so hellishly bushed!

Coley was never tired. Other people seemed to be tired for him. In every project which he had ever undertaken his adherents had flaked away at some stage, forgotten, like the jettisoned elements in a rocket flight. Hector Coley himself drove on to arrive at his object in perfect condition. But now he was tired, and he felt himself nearing exhaustion with his loss of blood and the battering he had taken.

There was just a chance, he thought, of a stop at Coleyville. The boy had evidently taken in the importance of that one. He'd postpone the final effort to get clear until Coleyville was reached.

He leant over the cold metal of which the log was made, and embraced it like a lover. The metal was cold and refreshing against the skin of face and chest. Through his blurring vision he saw again the great grey plain, and the approaching scissors intersection before Coleyville. Once again the smart little roadster ground to a peremptory halt at the crossing. Other cars halted behind it.

But the express did not this time slacken speed. It went through Coleyville at sixty. For a fleeting instant he saw again the maroon face of the guard, the giant blonde, the malevolence of the middle-aged schoolboy. Those waiting waited still. Those who had been waving waved on. Then Coleyville was gone, and the man on the log recognized that he would have to jump for it. He thought ahead.

Wistfully his mind passed over the swimming pool of the country club. If only that had been water! He winced at the appalling idea of crashing through glass.

But where else could he make it? Spring on to the roof of the tunnel, as they entered? But no, the mountain above was too sheer: it would be like flinging himself against a brick wall. Then he remembered the trees which overhung the long straight beyond. He'd been in the Pullman last time they'd gone under those. But he might be able to grab one and hang from it long enough to let the express pass beneath him.

He fainted away.

When he came to he found that the express was emerging from the tunnel. He wondered how many times he had made the circuit. Several times probably. Looking across the countryside from this high vantage point he could see on almost every track trains and cars travelling, east, west, south, north.

He felt a cold wind blowing now powerfully across the track. It was horrendous, roaring. It threatened to drag his very hair out by the roots. The shirt sleeves were flapping like mad, trapped seagulls. He twisted his head to face the blast and looked on at the final horror.

His son had quitted the control panel. He was now squatting, setting a fan on the long grey meadow of carpet. In the whirlwind everything light in the landscape was going over, the waving figures of the yokels and children, the flimsier structures of paper cottages. The station at Coley-

91

ville was collapsing, while the people on the platform waited patiently.

Brian smiled. Coley saw him smile.

Then, as he thought that he must be obliged to relinquish his hold and be blown away to destruction, the boy picked the fan up again, and placed it where it always was.

But he did not return to his seat at the control panel. He went out through the door, and shut it behind him. The noise as it slammed was like a shell exploding.

The express went down the long straight through the suspension bridge and towards the curve at the bottom and reached a hundred miles an hour. Coley watched the over-hanging branches of the trees sweep towards him. He climbed on to the logs and steadied himself with his feet braced against a knot to make this last leap. He realised that he would have to make it good the first time, and hoist himself well clear of the onrushing roofs of following coaches.

Red, yellow, brown, green, the trees suddenly showed.

He made his effort.

He felt the spines run through his hands. Then the branch broke, and he was jammed in the doorway of the next carriage.

He pulled a spine which had remained in his flesh clear, then lay there. He was broken. He waited for the express to derail.

But it did not derail. It swooped on the curve and screamed round it. Almost exuberantly it hurled itself at the next stretch running below the now abandoned control panel. Behind him he heard but did not see the last light trucks and petrol waggons go somersaulting off the track. For a moment there was a grinding check on the express: the wheels raced, then a link must have snapped and the wheels bit again. They surged forward.

The clatter as they started across the marshalling yard began again.

Coley got up quickly. The will which had devastated

92

board rooms, concentrated now in his tiny figure, was the only part of him which had not been reduced to a scale of one in three hundred. He remembered that before getting on to the express at the outset of this misconceived adventure he had sunk almost to his knees in the foam rubber ballast on which the track was laid. In the marshalling yard there was acres of it! He stepped back on the log-bearing truck and looked quickly about him.

'Foam-rubber,' he said to himself, 'not ballast.'

He flung himself out, as if into a feather bed.

He lay for a moment luxuriously. He watched the express disappear in the direction of shattered Coleyville. He sighed. What a close thing!

Downstairs, Brian was buckling on his raincoat. His mother watched him anxiously.

'I think your father would prefer it if just this once more you helped him with his trains. It's a bit late to go out.'

'No, he sent me away.'

His mother sighed. She looked forward to an uncomfortable scene with Hector when he should deign to reappear. He probably wouldn't even eat his dinner and then be even more bad tempered because he was hungry.

'Don't be out long, then.'

'I'm only going out to Billy's. We're going to watch for a hedgehog he says comes out at night in his garden.'

'All right then, but be sure to wrap up well.'

Coley hauled himself to his feet. He stood alone, a figure of flesh and blood in a world of fakes.

'I shall never play with them again, not after this,' he said, quietly.

It was a decision, but it was accurate also as a prophecy. A sibilant hiss was all he heard of the diesel before it struck him. It was travelling at only three miles an hour, or call it sixty.

It killed him.

Before he died, he thought, 'How wretched to die here

93

like this, tiny, probably not even found! They'll wonder whatever became of me.'

He wished he might have been out altogether of the tiny world which had proved to be too big for him. It was his dying wish.

No one doubted that it had been murder when Hector Coley was found stretched out across the toy world which had been his great hobby and pride. But so battered and bloodied and broken a figure could only have resulted from the attack of a maniac of prodigious, overwhelming strength.

'He was still playing with the models when he was surprised,' reported the Inspector, 'the current was on, and about ten of them had come to rest against his body. To be frank, though, he looked as if about ten real ones had hit him.'

ALEX HAMILTON

Acknowledgements

Acknowledgements are due to Robert Sheckley, Victor Gollancz Ltd and A. D. Peters and Co. for 'The Last Weapon' from *The People Trap*; Ray Bradbury, Hamish Hamilton Ltd, and Laurence Pollinger Ltd for 'The Wind' from *Dark Carnival*; Frederik Pohl and the E. J. Carnell Literary Agency for 'Small Lords' from *Day Million* (© 1956 by Columbia Publications Inc.); Arthur C. Clarke, Victor Gollancz Ltd and David Higham Associates Ltd for 'The Secret' from *The Wind from the Sun*; Alex Hamilton and Hutchinson Publishing Group Ltd for 'The Attic Express' from *Beam of Malice*; Damon Knight and the E. J. Carnell Literary Agency for 'Catch that Martian' (© 1952 by Galaxy Publishing Corporation).

Other Getaway Books

A Walk to See the King
Rony Robinson

Will and Martha might well have lived and died in
their Kent village without ever leaving it. But 1381
was the year of the great protest march. The year of
the Mad Priest. And the year of the scarred old soldier
—Wat Tyler. Will and Martha found their lives
caught up in the Walk. Separated, they are swept along
to London, and the King. They come to know that
the Walk cannot end happily for both Tyler and King,
or Will and Martha . . .

In 1381 Britain was a violent country, rigidly divided
between rich and poor. Instant justice was handed
down by whoever was in control, be it the King's army
or, momentarily, Wat Tyler's rabble. This novel
accurately reflects that world in a robust, exciting and
often moving account of two lives carried along on the
flood tide of a nation's anger, contrasted with the
struggle of a young King to assert himself as a person
instead of a symbol.